Gone Too Far Down That Road of No Return

INSPIRATIONAL CHRISTIAN PROSE POETRY BY

RICKY CLEMONS

PUBLISHED BY FIDELI PUBLISHING, INC.

ISBN: 978-1-970730-98-2

Published by

Fideli Publishing, Inc.
119 W. Morgan St.
Martinsville, IN 46151

www.FideliPublishing.com

Table of Contents

Gone Too Far Down that Road of No Return 1

I Look Back On My Life 7

We Can't Erase the Past 12

The Only Thing We Truly Own 20

Nobody Has it All Together All the Time 23

People Can Come Up with Their 25

It's Because of Jesus 27

The Road to Greatness 29

The Lord's Protection 30

This World 33

God's Holy Sanctuary 35

Spiritually Overweight 38

I am Calling on Jesus 41

No One Can Handle God 43

The Speed Limit of Life 45

It's So Easy to Believe 47

A One Day at a Time Journey 52

The Lord Will Not Let Us Off the Hook So Easily 55

Two Different Voices that Speak to Us in Our Minds 56

Nothing in this World will Always Last 59

We All are Human Beings 61

Lucifer Stopped Believing in God 65

The Prison Door of Sin 68

Jesus is the Only Way to Heaven 69

Love 73

Obey God 76

A Moment in Time...77

If We Pray and Ask the Lord for Wisdom....................79

The Holy Spirit..82

God is in Nature 83

The Power of Truth...85

That Will be Eternal, Except..87

There is Only One Afterlife 88

Jesus Is..89

Jesus is the Lamb of God 91

The Master of its 92

Who is Man? 93

Everybody Who Ever Lived 94

O Lord, All of Your Blessings are Great........................95

No One is Worthy...97

The Most Beautiful Woman in this World 99

In the Fullness of Time 100

God's Word Will Never Change 101

If it's Not One Thing, It's Another Thing..................... 102

Sometimes We Can Move Too Fast.............................. 103

My Ignorance 104

Just Downright No Good 105

I Don't Have the Strength to Walk on My Own 106

It's So Easy 107

Lost in Space 108

Never Satisfied 109

Only I Can Have My 110

Through All of My Regrets 113

You and I will Usually Want To 114

Powerful Words 115

True Happiness 116

Only Jesus can Create a New World 118

Can We Understand? 120

Can't Do More 123

The Greatest Reward 125

In Your Hands, O Lord 127

There is a Decree from Heaven 128

A New Creature in Jesus Christ 130

Being Married to Jesus 132

If 135

The Mysteries of Life 138

The Show-Offs 140

Quietness 142

There is No Way to Get Around the Lord's Holy Word 143

In the Spiritual Deep Sleep 146

The Big Wheels of Time 149

Believe in Jesus Christ 150

Jesus is the Same Jesus Every Day 152

Jesus Truly Knows and the Devil Truly Knows 154

Jesus says, "If you love Me, you will keep My Commandments" 156

There is No Time Left 158

Who Can Understand God's Decisions? 160

God's Precious Jewels 162

We Have to get Tough with the Devil 163

You and I Must Go Through Some Hardships 164

If Your Heart is Broken into a Thousand Pieces 166

Across the Countless Galaxies 168

Will Move On Into 170

The Devil's Most Busy Day 172

If God was Not Miraculous 175

The Truth is the Best Thing 177

If You and I Make it to Heaven 179

Prayer is a Lifestyle for Every Christian 181

Gone Too Far
Down that Road of No Return

There are many people who have gone too far down that road of no return back to the Lord.

They once drank the drink of the spiritual milk and ate the spiritual meat of the Lord who filled them up with the delicious truth of His holy word, but they began to choose to eat the materialistic, corrupt food of the world and they strayed away to the point of no return back to the Lord.

There are many people who have gone too far down that road of no return back to the Lord because they got so caught up in the majestic, scenic views of the wisdom of the world that they kept their eyes on and it spiritually blinded them down that road of no return back to Jesus.

There are many people who have gone too far down that road of no return back to the Lord.

There are many people who have gone too far down that road of no return back to the Lord because they were mesmerized by the fame of the world that they saw down that road and that took their hearts so far away from Jesus.

There are many people who have gone too far down that road of no return back to the Lord Jesus Christ because they enjoyed the pleasures of living in their sins to go down that road of no return back to the Lord who takes no pleasure in destroying what He created to give Him all the glory and praise.

There are many people who have gone too far down that road of no return back to the Lord, and they'd be better off never having been born than to once have worshipped the Lord in His holy tabernacle and then left the church like it never existed for them.

Many people who have never been to church are better off for the Lord to steer them down His road that leads to eternal life than those who once lived for Jesus and then pushed Jesus out of their lives being like they were throwing away a billion dollars in a trash dump — that's something a fool wouldn't even think about doing.

There are many people who have gone too far down that road of no return back to Jesus even in the household of faith where there are church folks who have no faith in Jesus and believe that their works can entitle them to have favor with God.

There are many people who have gone too far down that road of no return back to Jesus who they once prayed to and the Lord answered their prayers, but they used their answered prayers in the wrong way to make themselves look like they worked everything out in their lives that were a big mess that Jesus worked out for them.

There are many people who have gone too far down that road of no return and will surely try to take you and me down that road with them.

Those who have gone down that road are very selfish because that road has taken them too far away from the Lord.

There are many people who have gone too far down that road of no return back to Jesus and they don't see it and will call on Jesus' name in vain and have no guilt or shame about turning their backs on Jesus.

You and I must make our calling very sure in Jesus and not just go through the motions of going to church without having a true change in our hearts to humble ourselves before the Lord.

You and I are not exempt from going down that road of no return back to Jesus, and that can happen right in the church because you and I are not exempt from Jesus saying to us, "Depart from Me, I never knew you."

We can anchor ourselves in the gospel of Jesus Christ because Jesus gave us all a free will to choose not to go down that road of no return back to Him.

That road is a very dangerous spiritual road that leads us to total darkness and causes us to spiritually murder our own souls so that we end up in the second resurrection for Jesus' angels to throw us in the lake of fire where that road ends with eternal death.

Those who have gone down that road of no return back to Jesus have grieved the Holy Spirit so much that the Holy Spirit no longer speaks to their heart and they are spiritually dead, even in the church where we can hold onto unconfessed and unrepentant sins and be lost right in the church.

That road of no return back to Jesus can be right in the church if we go there with a heart set on pushing Jesus away from us and believe that we are like angels of light when we are surely darkness before the Lord Jesus Christ who no one can ever fool outside the church and inside the church.

Going down that road of no return back to Jesus is to die and be lost in our sins that we can only confess and repent of while being alive, because there is no return back to Jesus in the grave.

The dead know nothing and can do nothing to get in contact with the living who can choose not to go down that road of no return back to Jesus.

Many people have gone too far down that road of no return back to Jesus and many people who are still in the church are going down that road too.

There are many people alive today who never heard about Jesus, yet they're better off than those traveling that road of no return back to Jesus.

They are definitely better off than you and me if we turn our backs on Jesus and live in darkness for the rest of our lives.

Going too far down that road of no return back to Jesus will bring tears to God's eyes because it will be God's strange act to even cast Lucifer and his fallen angels into fire and brimstone that is surely not meant for you and me to be thrown into because God is love and will return anyone back to His Son, Jesus Christ, if we repent and live for Jesus.

God's grace is sufficient to be greater than our sins, but grace can't interfere with anyone's free will choice.

God's grace can't stop anyone from choosing to go too far down that road of no return back to His only begotten son, Jesus Christ, who lives forever beyond that road of no return back to Him.

Lucifer and his angels had their chance to return back to Jesus, but they refused to do that and went too far down that road of no return, making hell their destiny—just as many people, even in the church, also do today.

Even though the church is Jesus' bride, there are also tares in the church and Jesus truly knows those who have gone too far down that road of no return back to Him because they only go through the motions and pretend to love Jesus so they give off a good outward appearance.

You and I must make our calling very sure in Jesus Christ, because we have no shortcuts to take to get by Jesus who is the only one to save us from our sins.

Many people have gone too far down that road of no return back to Jesus and are dead in their graves because they died being lost in their sins—they tried to take too many short cuts to avoid Jesus due to their false doctrines.

They ended up being lost right in the church because they turned their backs on Jesus and did their own will, causing them to go too far down that road of no return back to Jesus.

Let's you and me not make that same big eternal mistake, because Jesus is the love of God who no one can out-love.

God gives you and me so many chances to choose to not go too far down that road of no return back to Jesus, who we can turn our backs on even in our thoughts before we speak one word.

Only the Lord Jesus Christ knows all who have gone too far down that road of no return back to Him, and only Jesus knows all who are on their way down that road of no return back to Him.

Jesus is our only living road that is never too far down for anyone to not return back to Him who has countless numbers of His holy saints going to heaven where there is no return back to this old, sinful world that will one day pass away with all those who have gone too far down that road of no return back to Jesus.

You and I are vulnerable and could make that choice to go too far down that road of no return back to Jesus right in the church if we don't keep our eyes on Jesus, to keep our eyes on imperfect people who have sins to confess and repent of unto Jesus Christ.

Sanctification is a lifetime process for everyone in the church.

You and I can't just say once we're saved we're always saved, because it is a one day at a time process to be saved in Jesus.

Going too far down that road of no return back to Jesus starts with making excuses for our sins as a daily routine—this causes the Holy Spirit to slowly move away from us and we will no longer hear His sweet, quiet voice speaking to our hearts telling us to love and obey Jesus who is never too far away from us to save us from our sins.

We can push Jesus far away from us right in the church and go too far down that road of no return back to Jesus while sitting right there in the church pews.

Judas was one of Jesus' disciples but he went too far down that road of no return because Judas was right in the church when he turned his back on Jesus and betrayed him for 30 pieces of silver as well as with a kiss on Jesus' cheek.

Judas hung himself because he realized he would have been better off to never have been born than to betray Jesus.

We church folks are not exempted from going too far down that road of no return back to the Lord Jesus Christ.

Hell would be so happy to vanish us away without a trace in fire and brimstone where we can't return back to Jesus.

Anyone who rejects God's salvation in His Son, Jesus Christ, has gone too far down that road of no return back to Jesus.

Many church folks believe that their ministry works can save them, but that makes them worse off than an unbeliever who has a better chance to be saved in Jesus like the thief on the cross who asked Jesus to remember him as he hung on his cross beside Jesus.

Jesus' response to the thief was to accept him into paradise forever beyond going too far down that road of no return.

Book of Hebrews 6:4-6

I Look Back On My Life

I look back on my life and I thank You, O Lord, for humbling me by allowing me to lose my mind from the bad drugs that I used.

O Lord, I thank You for humbling me in order to save my soul from being lost in my sins that I was living in so proudly and ignorantly, especially about You, O Lord.

O Lord, you allowed me to lose my mind, even though it broke Your heart.

You knew that losing my mind was the only way You could humble me and break me from my false pride that You didn't let me die in to give me a second chance to repent and turn to You, O Lord.

O Lord, You gave me a second chance in my broken down mind and you mended me and put me back together through my lost years when I missed out on sanity through my own bad choices.

O Lord, I look back on my past life and know that because of Your love for me I can truly see today that You humbled me because it was the best way to make me see how I was so frail without You being first in my life.

I look back on my life and I truly see what a fool I was for believing I was invincible and that nothing bad could ever happen to me.

What I didn't know then was I was on my way to hell.

I look back on my life and I am so glad today that You, O Lord, humbled me to save my soul from being lost in my sins.

I was so very ignorant of that, but You, O Lord, foresaw it and it hurt Your heart to allow me to lose my mind, even though it was the best thing that could have happened to me.

Today, I know true sanity is loving You and keeping Your holy laws.

I truly know today that spiritual healing is beyond any mental, emotional, psychological and physical healing.

I look back on my life today and see that the doctors' medicine couldn't heal me spiritually, which was what I needed most.

When I look back on my life today, I truly see that Jesus had to humble me to keep me from destroying myself in my false pride.

When I was in my right mind and could do normal daily things, I went overboard and believed that I was almighty and could do whatever I wanted to do.

The Lord is merciful to allow me to look back on my life that belonged to Him and not me, even though I believed I was my own master and that no one else could tell me how to live my life.

I was so ignorant and didn't care to see that I was on the road to self-destruction, so, O Lord, You had to humble me because You didn't want me to be lost in my sins.

I am so blessed to be in my right mind today, that I truly know that I don't deserve from the Lord Jesus Christ who is perfect in all of His ways of doing things.

Jesus can mold and shape any one of us to be without excuse to keep our mind on Him.

I look back on my life today and I see nothing that the Lord didn't do for me to be sane.

Today I truly know that Jesus loves me more than I can ever imagine in my lifetime.

No one is worthy to tell me to forget about my past life that no one but Jesus brought me through.

Only Jesus is worthy to move my life on into His reasons for me to always trust Him to be right and lead me to Mount Calvary where He foreknew all of my life troubles and humbled Himself unto the insanity of death and rose from the grave to save me from my sins.

I look back on my life and I remember that the military psychiatrist told me I would never be able to socialize again, but my Lord Jesus Christ proved him to be so wrong.

The psychiatrist's medicine that I take is only a small thing to help me functional normally in my life that I love to live unto the Lord who has cleansed me of my past sins that no psychiatrist's medicine can ever cleanse.

I look back on my life and I know today that the Lord has made me spiritually well in my mind because the psychiatrist's medicine has no power to keep me from living in sin, which is crazy to God.

The doctor's medicine can't cleanse anyone from their sins — only Jesus can do that if we confess and repent and turn to Jesus.

There are many people who never lose their minds and are doing crazy things that many people who have lost their minds would not do.

Just because someone loses their mind does not mean that he or she is evil.

Many people who are functioning in their normal minds are doing a lot of evil things that they believe to be normal things to do.

Most of the criminals in the prisons, both male and female, have never lost their minds and many of them are very intelligent, but they won't think twice about taking someone's life.

I look back on my life and I truly understand today that the Lord allowed me to lose my mind to protect me from an early grave that I was digging down in for living a rebellious life that would have taken me to the place of no returning back to the Lord.

The Lord stepped in on time to stop me from destroying myself to see this day that I don't deserve to have a spiritual mind unto the Lord.

You and I can lose our minds in God's holy word and we will never regret being crazy for Jesus, who is forever sane to save us from being lost in our crazy sins that many people believe to be sane for them to live in day by day.

I am truly sane today because of knowing and living by God's holy word that scoffers and atheists believe to have been written by delusional men who had lost their minds that were completely sane for an unseen God to dwell in.

I look back on my life and truly thank the Lord for making me humble the hard way.

Many people might think this is a strange thing to say, but losing my mind is so much better than being dead and lost in my sins, which would mean my chances ran out to repent and turn to Jesus, who made me sane to write this to hopefully encourage others to believe in Jesus.

The worst kind of mind to lose is your spiritual mind, which sends you straying away from the Lord even though you can talk normal and act normal on the outside, which even a serial killer can do.

Many people have lost their spiritual minds right in the church, like Jim Jones and David Koresh and so on.

It's better for people who are mentally ill to recover their right minds by repenting and turning to Jesus.

I look back on my life and I truly see what a fool I was before I lost my mind from using bad drugs when I was in the military.

If I had lost my life fighting in a war at that time, my death would have been eternal.

The Lord showed His miraculous mercy on me and didn't let me stay lost in my mind for the rest of my life, because He had predestined to save the uttermost sinner like me from being lost in my sins.

No one can be so lost in their mind that Jesus can't restore them back to sanity.

I am proof of that, just like King Nebuchadnezzar whose lost mind was restored by God, even though King Nebuchadnezzar believed he was invincible and like God.

God humbled him down the hard way and made him eat grass like an ox for seven years.

I truly believe today that if I had a relationship with the Lord before I joined the military, then I would not have used those bad drugs.

I chose drugs to be my master and that caused me to lose my mind, but if I'd had a relationship with God, then it would have been impossible for me to serve two masters at the same time and my mind would not have been lost.

Who can go insane when they have a relationship with Jesus Christ?

No true Christian can go insane when they love Jesus and keep His Commandments, but anyone can go insane if they love using bad drugs.

I look back on my life today and I truly see that Jesus suffered long for me to be sane in my mind.

Many people in the past believed if you lost your mind then you were crazy and evil, but because of the advanced medical knowledge today many people know that having a mental illness doesn't mean that you're crazy or evil.

They just need to get some medical treatment to get their minds back to normal daily living.

The medical field originates from the Lord Jesus Christ, who healed many people in body and mind when He lived in this world with no sin in His flesh that people could touch and be healed.

When I lost my mind many years ago, I lost most of my memory to be like I had Alzheimer's.

Everything that I had learned in school and in the military was pretty much gone from my memory.

It's a miracle to me to be able to write this today.

The Lord blessed the military psychiatrist's medicine to help bring most of my memory back to me.

The Lord takes no pleasure to humble anyone who rebels against Him.

It's like the Lord's last reason for Him to humble anyone who is proud and arrogant.

I look back on my life and I truly see many chances that God gave to me to see this day that only God is worthy to put a too late to be saved time on all who have sinned and fallen short of the glory of God.

We Can't Erase the Past

We can't erase the past like it never existed because the past will affect the present and the future.

No one in their right mind wants to erase their deceased loved one from their memory so no one truly wants to erase the past.

We can't erase the past that we lived in with our good days and bad days that the Lord allowed us to all experience for His reasons to help us to be sure about making Him our choice without a doubt, even though many of us doubted Jesus in the past.

We can't erase the past like it never existed in our lives, because the past has a lot to do with the way we are today, whether we were Christians in the past or not Christians in the past that did exist.

We can't erase the past like it never existed in our lives, because who in their right mind would want to forget that it was the Lord who spared their life from death so many times in the past.

Only a fool would pretend like that never happened to not exist and will keep it a secret like they brought themselves this far to see this present day.

Many Christians today want to forget their past life like it never existed, but they love to preach to people and teach people about the bible that is all about the past, going back thousands of years of good and bad people existing in this world.

Many Christians want to erase their past lives like they never lived them doing their own will, but they love to read the bible that was written about many people doing their own will before doing the Lord's will.

The people who want to erase the past like it never existed need to think about what it would be like if there was no past.

If this happened, then especially the bible would have no proof to give to us about how we came into existence and how we are here in the present.

If we only live in the present and erase the past in our lives like it never existed, then we are erasing ourselves like we don't exist.

No one in their right mind would want to do that!

The voice of the bible prophecy speaks to us from the past and no true Christian would want to erase it like it never existed.

It goes to show that our past obeyed God's voice to bring us into the present.

The future can't reason with God for our present to not one day be our past that's there to encourage the next generation to love Jesus and keep His Commandments.

You and I can't erase our past lives like they didn't exist because there may have been some Christian people who we just didn't know who prayed for you and me in our past lives and helped you and me be alive today to believe in Jesus Christ and be saved.

Many people will say that it's all in the past, but it's the past that shapes the present and the future that we can read about in the bible.

The prophets of God in the past predicted what will happen in the future to warn us to repent and turn to Jesus who is coming back again, and no one knows the hour for His return except God.

We love to remember the good things that happened to us in our past lives, but we don't want to remember the bad things that happened to us in our past lives.

The Lord uses these things for our good to be a witness of Him in giving our testimonies to especially unbelievers who need to see our renewed lives that the reality of the past shouts with joy over because we are no longer that old carnal-minded creature rebelling against the God of the past, present and future.

No one can erase the past history in this world because God allowed that to happen to teach us not to repeat past mistakes, especially the bad history that only the wicked will repeat, according to the bible prophecy that no one can erase.

No one can erase the past, no matter how educated they are, no matter how prosperous they are, and no matter how close they are to Jesus who came into this world in the past and died on the cross to save us from our sins in the past, thousands of years ago.

This is vital to every Christian who knows today that Jesus Christ rose from the grave with victory over death that will repeat the past for the wicked to one day receive eternal death.

It's not a sin to think or talk about the bad things we did in our past lives, as long as we thank the Lord and give testimonies about the Lord showing His great mercy on us and giving us a second chance to repent and turn to Him.

Our past lives can't override this second chance and it can't stop us from encouraging someone to live for the Lord.

There are so-called Christians who will detest our past life and call it a curse instead of a blessing to someone who may need to hear our testimonies about the Lord giving us a second chance to live for Him in this present day and win a lost soul to Him.

We can't erase the past like it's invisible like the air we breathe in and out of our nostrils — we cannot live without air.

We also can't live without the past that breathes learning from our past mistakes so we can wise up and obey the Lord, who was there with us in our past lives when we just didn't know that the Lord was watching over us.

We have no reason to believe that the past has nothing worthwhile for us and we should just erase it from our minds instead of giving Jesus the thanks, glory and praise for helping us overcome our past deficiencies.

We cannot just pretend like those deficiencies never existed in our lives because we're so strong in the Lord today, even though it's easy for us to want to overlook the past and the fact that Jesus brought us through the past when we were trapped in our sins.

Only Jesus is worthy to erase the past like it never existed, and one day Jesus will erase the past from us forever and ever that only He can do.

We can easily live our lives like the past never existed, but we are only fooling ourselves — not God.

God uses the good and bad from our past for His holy purpose, and no one can rise above God and say He's wrong about anything in our past, present and future.

God will use this to serve His holy purpose that is always right for everyone to be in, beyond the sun and under the sun.

King Solomon said there is nothing new under the sun, which only goes to show that everything going on today has already happened before in the past.

From the beginning of life in this world, there has always been the same holy law of God and the immorality that was very present in the past.

When Jesus lived in this world without sin in His flesh, Jesus didn't erase the past to make Himself the second Adam to save us from the sins that the first Adam brought upon us all to be born in.

Jesus didn't repeat the disobedience to God like the first Adam did in the Garden of Eden.

Jesus created this world that was perfect in the past that we Christians don't want to ever erase like it never happened, because we are looking forward to living in a new perfect world one day with Jesus.

Jesus didn't erase the rebellion of the fallen angels like they never rebelled against God, who will one day cast them into the lake of fire that He created for the fallen angels.

Why would any human being want to erase the past as if our past life never existed?

We can want to erase the past to make it seem as if we have always been the same holy and righteous man or woman and no change of life exists for us because we are perfect in every word we said and every thing we did so that our past life looks so blameless before others, especially unbelievers.

They miss the point of the whole purpose of Jesus washing us clean in His blood that He shed on the cross for our sins.

Jesus did this so we could live a renewed life in Him and our past lives could act as a testimony to one another that it was Jesus who showed His mercy on us and didn't let us die in our sins so that we could live in this present day and give Him all the thanks, glory and praise for allowing us to live beyond our past that didn't care if we died in our sins.

Even children who are born and raised up in a Christian home have a past life of not always being like Jesus, who suffers long with every living soul to be saved in Him who is the only One who lived a past perfect life with no sin in His flesh so he could erase our past, present and future sins.

Like King Solomon said thousands of years ago, "there is nothing new under the sun," meaning the past is the past and we can't erase the past.

That King Solomon was the wisest man who ever lived.

Without the past, there would be no present and future because God is the past, present and future, and no one can erase God, who is self-existence and uses the past for His glory.

All life here on earth began in the past that we can't erase like it never existed.

If we try to erase the past, it's like we are erasing ourselves because we are here today because of the past generations of people called our ancestors who existed before you and me here in the present day and time.

Trying to erase the past is like trying to erase God, who originated the past here on earth to give us the good and bad to look back on so we will know that God has always been in everyone's past lives.

No one has a good excuse to try to erase the past that God uses to teach us that nothing gets by Him to keep us from believing in His Son, Jesus Christ, to be saved.

It's so easy to say that you need to get beyond the past, but God uses the past to direct our present life, especially in living for Him who the devil hates the most.

God uses our past life for our good, while the devil uses our past life for our bad.

We can't erase our past life like we never had a past life that was bad and because it was bad, we want to forget it.

The devil wants us to forget and not use our past life's bad experiences to encourage someone else to be thankful unto Jesus for giving up His life on the cross in our place.

We crucify Jesus over and over again by wanting to erase the past.

Jesus didn't erase what He went through to save us from our sins and to make our pleas before God in the heavenly courtroom.

We all truly deserve to have a bad past, present and future life for being born in sin against God who the devil hates to see spearhead our past lives into our glorious and changed renewed life in Jesus Christ, who is worthy for us to bow down our past, present and future life unto.

Moving on beyond our past lives means accepting our past lives and give them to Jesus Christ.

Anyone who is in denial about their bad past life would be better off with their tongue cut out of their mouth so they can't talk about erasing their past life that only the Lord can bless to be a good example for the present and future.

The past is all about the present and future for everyone to know from the past bible prophecies letting us know what will happen in these last days here on earth.

The past was all about Jesus Christ, who would crush the devil's head and take back the dominion over the earth that the first Adam gave up to the devil way back in the past thousands of years ago.

No one can erase that like it never happened and get by God to get away with their false belief.

We can't erase the past like it never existed and we true Christians know that without the past prophets of God and disciples of Jesus Christ there would be no present day Christian living.

Time on earth is short and Jesus is coming back in the hour that no one knows but God.

We can't erase the past kings like they never existed.

We can't erase the past kingdoms like they never existed.

We can't erase the past wars like they never existed.

We can't erase the past genocides like they never existed.

We can't erase the past slavery like it never existed.

We can't erase the past presidents of the United States of America like they never existed.

We can't erase the past civil rights leaders like they never existed.

We can't erase anything that God allowed to happen for His reasons, which we can't erase from the past, present and future.

We can't erase the past seconds, minutes, hours, days, weeks, months and years like they never existed when they all add up to only the Lord keeping us alive beyond our past lives that the Lord used to mold and shape our present so we have no excuse to not live for Him who gave the past, present and future a place to rest their case in throughout eternity.

The only thing that can be erased from the past is our past sins that only Jesus can erase like they never existed if we confess and repent of our past sins that will only exist to you and me and those who know how we lived a past, sinful life.

Jesus erases our past sins to be no history to Him when the sins of many people are written in books to even be a best-seller.

We can't erase the past like it never existed when wise people will not repeat the past bad history as well as their past sins.

We can't erase the past like it never existed when there is only one thing in the past that Jesus will erase like it never existed to him, and that is our past sins for us to not repeat.

There are those in our lives who are not saved in Jesus and they just don't really care about us repeating our past sins because there is no change in them to want to live for Jesus.

We can't erase the past like it never existed but we can give everything in the past to Jesus, who was there in the past for everyone in the past to repent and turn to Him as well as Jesus being in the present and in the future for everyone to repent and turn to Him before it's too late.

Jesus has given everyone time in the past to repent and turn to Him who walked and talked with Adam and Eve in the perfect Garden of Eden.

Jesus gives time to everyone who is alive today to repent and turn to Him who will erase our past and present sins like they never existed to Him.

We know that babies and immature little children don't know right from wrong, and the same is true for many mentally challenged teenagers and adults who Jesus will not hold accountable for their sins that Jesus will erase like they never existed to Him.

Only Jesus is worthy to erase the past because only Jesus lived in this world with no sin in His flesh in the past, thousands of years ago, which is like only a few days ago to God.

Whatever Jesus erases isn't impossible to bring back to God for review.

The Only Thing We Truly Own

The only thing we truly own is our God-given free will to choose right from wrong.

The only thing we truly own is our God-given free will to choose to do good or evil.

The only thing we truly own is our God-given free will to also choose to think good thoughts or bad thoughts.

The only thing we truly own is our God-given free will to choose to say good words or bad words.

We don't even own our bodies because they belong to the Lord to live in us if we choose to let Him live in us, and if we don't choose to let Jesus live in us He still owns our bodies but not our free will to choose.

We came into this world with nothing and we will leave this world with nothing but our free will that will show and tell our destiny by the choices we make in the land of the living.

The only thing we truly own is our God-given free will to choose, which the dead can't do in the grave.

Many people will carry themselves like they own the material things in this world that belongs to Jesus, not us.

We only own our God-given free will to choose to live or die for what we choose to believe in.

Many people will carry themselves like they own all the world until death knocks on their door and proves to them that they can only own their free will to choose to die believing the truth that they don't own this world.

The only thing we truly own is our God-given free will to choose, which is the greatest thing to call our own because only our choices can guarantee us eternal wealth for choosing to believe in Jesus Christ.

If we claim to own anything else in this world there is no guarantee in the temporary things in this world that will pass away one day.

Our God-given free will to choose is the only thing that we own and it will get us into heaven if we choose to love and obey Jesus.

We can always feel good about wanting to own anything in this world where material things can burden us and keep us down for calling them our own, when we only own our free will to choose.

Even a fool will not find this ownership to be a burden and will choose freely from day to day.

It goes to show that God is nothing but love forever and ever with no selfishness in Him to want to control you and me who he gave a free will to choose that the devil has no control over.

For you and me to believe that the devil made us say something or do something against our God-given free will to choose freely is foolish.

No one can blame God or the devil if we are lost in hell because it will be our own choosing in the land of the living that put us there.

We own our God-given free will, not God or the devil.

They can't force us to think, say or do anything that we don't want to think, say or do.

God has given us all the free will to choose, and we truly own that.

The devil can't take that free will away from us, but he can tempt us to stray away from God.

We have to call on Jesus and live for Jesus who chose to become like us in the flesh to relate to us and redeem us back to God.

It doesn't take much effort to choose to live for the devil.

Just imagine if the devil had the power to control us and make us do nothing but evil every day, and we would not be able to choose to say or do anything good.

We can truly thank God for also being so very fair to the human race by giving us a free will to call our own in this world where one day Jesus will stand up and say that it is finished.

The righteous will remain righteous and the wicked will remain wicked because of their own choosing.

We each can so freely choose to live for Jesus or the devil, who has no control over the choices we make.

If we choose to believe in Jesus Christ, the Holy Spirit will have our backs and help us to live for Jesus, when the devil will only have our backs to make us lost in our sins for choosing to live for him.

The devil truly knows that our God-given free will to choose is a big problem for him because he knows that we can choose to love and obey Jesus and be saved.

Nobody Has it All Together All the Time

Nobody in this world has it all together all the time.

Nobody in the church has it all together all the time.

Abraham didn't have it all together all the time because he told the Egyptians that Sarah was his sister and not his wife to keep from getting killed by the Egyptians who God would have protected him from if he had told them that Sarah was his wife.

Elijah didn't have it all together all the time because he ran away from Jezebel who God would have protected him from.

Moses didn't have it all together all the time because he hit the rock when God told him to speak to the rock and water would come out for the people to drink.

Peter didn't have it all together all the time because he denied Jesus three times, saying that he didn't know Jesus when someone asked him if he was one of Jesus' disciples.

No one has it all together all the time because we all were born in sin to not have ourselves together all the time.

We need to pray without ceasing and ask the Lord to give us His Holy Spirit who we need all the time.

No matter how holy and righteous someone may seem to be in church, no one is perfect to have no sins to confess and repent of unto the Lord.

Only Jesus had it all together all the time when He lived in this sinful world with no sins in His flesh because Jesus was not born in sin but was born of the Holy Spirit from His Heavenly Father, God.

Because Jesus had it all together all the time, He was worthy to save us from our sins that cause us to not have it all together all the time, even in the church.

The disciples didn't have it all together all the time, especially when they were in the storm that rocked their boat, but Jesus calmed the storm that knew that only Jesus had Himself all together all the time.

People Can Come Up with Their

People can come up with their theories, but if Jesus is not in them then they're just a bunch of confusion.

People can come up with their truths, but if Jesus is not in them then they're just a bunch of disagreements.

People can come up with their votes, but if Jesus is not in them then they're just a bunch of strife.

People can come up with their arguments, but if Jesus isn't in them then they're just a bunch of headaches.

People can come up with their decisions, but if Jesus is not in them then they're just a bunch of foolishness.

People can come up with their job titles, but if Jesus is not in them then they're just a bunch of worthlessness.

People can come up with their achievements, but if Jesus is not in them then they're just a bunch of hazardous waste.

People can come up with their ideas, but if Jesus is not in them then they're just a bunch of failures.

People can come up with their educated guesses, but if Jesus is not in them then they're just a bunch of bubbles.

People can come up with their ways of doing things, but if Jesus is not in them then they're just a bunch of waywardness.

People can come up with their words to say, but if Jesus is not in them then they're just a bunch of loose screws.

People can come up with their beliefs, but if Jesus is not in them then they're just a bunch of lost causes.

People can come up with their ways of feeling good, but if Jesus is not in them then they're just a bunch of lack of fulfillment.

People can come up with their creativity, but if Jesus is not in it then it's just a bunch of cannon balls.

People can come up with their wisdom, but if Jesus is not in it then it's just a bunch of water running down a drain.

People can come up with their diets, but if Jesus is not in them then they're just a bunch of health deficiencies.

People can come up with their plans, but if Jesus is not in them then they're just a bunch of obstacles.

The Pharisees and chief priests believed that they were so righteous without putting Jesus in their lives, but that was a bunch of deception for rejecting Jesus.

People can come up with all kinds of things, but if Jesus is not in them then they're just a bunch of smoke.

People can come up with their rights and wrongs, but if Jesus is not in them then they're just a bunch of evils.

People can come up with their laws, but if Jesus is not in them then they're just a bunch of burdens.

People can come up with their love but if Jesus is not in it then it's just a bunch of favoritism.

One day soon, Jesus will come up with coming back again on the clouds of glory that will be a bunch of holy angels taking all the holy saints up in the sky to Jesus, who will give all the holy saints a bunch of eternal life in heaven.

Church folks can come up with their programs in the church, but if Jesus is not in them then they're just a bunch of waste of time in the church.

The disciples had come up with their beliefs but they were just a bunch of lies, because Jesus had told them that this world is not His kingdom.

It's Because of Jesus

It's because of Jesus if I live to see another day, not because of luck.

It's because of Jesus if something good comes my way, not because of any horoscope.

It's because of Jesus if I don't get injured in a car accident, not because of luck.

It's because of Jesus if my marriage lasts a lifetime, not because of any horoscope.

It's because of Jesus if I get a good night's sleep, not because of magic.

It's because of Jesus if I live one hundred years, not because of magic.

It's because of Jesus if I get rich, not because of any horoscope.

It's because of Jesus if I control my tongue, not because of any wish.

One day in the afternoon I went to the post office, and when I entered the post office there were five people standing in line ahead of me.

I could not help but to overhear a man saying to a woman that he believes in horoscopes.

When I heard those words, I wanted to interrupt them to say that I believe in Jesus Christ, but the Holy Spirit spoke to me and said to keep my mouth closed.

I remembered before I walked into the post office I had prayed and asked the Lord to give me the wisdom to know what to say and know what not to say.

The Lord answered my prayer and told me not to say anything when I heard what that man said to that woman he didn't know.

He also said to that woman that he and his wife had been married for fifty years because of his belief in horoscopes.

He believed that the horoscope brought them together.

The Holy Spirit spoke to me and said, "You can't judge him for what he believes because you don't know how he was raised and what he has been through in his life."

The devil had tried to tempt me into interrupting that man and woman's conversation in the post office.

I was glad I listened to the Holy Spirit and kept my mouth closed, because the woman spoke up and told the man she didn't believe in horoscopes.

The Lord winks His eye at people's ignorance.

There was a time in my life when I believed in horoscopes too, and the Lord winked His eye at my ignorance when I just didn't know any better.

Now I know it's because of Jesus Christ that good things can happen, even to ignorant people.

The Lord sends His rain down and also causes the sun to shine; both are good things from the Lord, not from any horoscope, luck, magic or wish.

The Road to Greatness

The road to greatness is a lonely road to walk down to get to Jesus, who is the totality of greatness to all the angels in heaven.

The road to greatness is to humble ourselves unto the Lord Jesus Christ every day, since that greatness is truly all about being like Jesus.

Greatness in this sinful world can come and go, but Jesus is eternal greatness who lives forever and that is greatness to the unfallen worlds.

Here in this world, we usually think greatness is being a millionaire or billionaire.

Here in this world, we usually think greatness is being famous or being a genius.

Here in this world, we usually think greatness is being a supermodel or President of the United States.

Here in this world, we usually think greatness is making a new discovery or inventing something.

Here in this world, we usually think greatness is having a best-selling book and getting rich.

Here in this world, we usually think greatness is having our own business or being a war veteran.

Here in this world, we usually think greatness is being a pilot or a preacher.

Here in this world, we usually think greatness is being an athlete or a whiz kid.

Here in this world, we usually thing greatness is being a hero or a doctor or a surgeon.

True greatness is Jesus Christ, who created all things seen and unseen.

We will never see or know what greatness really is until we see Jesus Christ on the clouds of glory with all of His angels on that great day for all the saints to see and live forever with Jesus in heaven.

The Lord's Protection

The Lord's protection is all we truly have from day to day because you and I can't truly protect ourselves from danger and harm and death.

You can be a great martial artist and can't truly protect yourself from death that can come to you in over a thousand ways.

You can be a top-notch Navy Seal and can't truly protect yourself from death that can catch you off of your guard at any time of the day and night.

You can be the best Marine and can't truly protect yourself from death that can come upon you even after the war is over.

You can be a fighter pilot hitting so many targets and you can't truly protect yourself from death that can sneak up on you even as a little parasite that can get in your bloodstream and kill you.

The Lord's miraculous protection is all that we truly have from day to day.

I had a great friend who was a fighter jet pilot who knocked out some enemy jets in the Vietnam War.

He was a Puerto Rican man from Buffalo, New York, who had been paralyzed in a car accident and was in a hospital bed at the Veteran's Hospital the last time I visited him.

He said he couldn't believe this happened to him while he was off duty, instead of being hit by an enemy fighter jet.

This just shows that he couldn't protect himself while driving on the road where it was supposed to be safer than fighting the enemy in his jet up in the sky.

The Lord's protection is all that you and I truly have from day to day.

Without the Lord's almighty protection upon us, the devil will surely take us out of the land of the living.

Many of us even have loved ones who got killed at a very young age and we don't understand why the Lord didn't protect them from death and going to an early grave.

All of us who are still alive right now are truly alive because of the Lord's protection.

We can't truly protect ourselves from death that so many people of every age get swallowed down into its belly of no return day after day.

Who can truly keep themselves alive without the Lord's protection?

The Lord's protection is all that we truly have.

Every soldier who makes it back home alive is truly alive because of the Lord's protection upon them beyond their vigorous combat training.

Many soldiers on the battlefields know without a doubt that the Lord protected them from death when they believed that they would be killed.

Our only sure protection is from the Lord.

Many people have confessed that death looked at them straight in their eyes and was so ready to take them out in the blink of an eye, but the Lord stepped in and spared them from death.

When people live through a terrible plane crash, a terrible pile-up car accident, a monster hurricane, a terrible flood, a terrible wildfire, and even those who lived through the Corona virus, lived because of the Lord's protection upon them.

The Lord's protection is all that we truly have from day to day to protect us from death, which is our number-one enemy.

Death takes us out of the land of the living if the Lord allows it, no matter how many sophisticated weapons of war any nation has.

The Lord's all-powerful protection is all that we truly have against the devil, who would have destroyed every human being in the world over a thousand years ago if God had not protected man's salvation by giving His Son, Jesus Christ, to save all men from their sins.

If we truly believe that we can protect ourselves from death and believe that we are die-hards, then a massive earthquake will surely show us how defenseless we are.

That earthquake could crush us down under man-made houses and buildings that are no true protection for us against death.

The only true protection that we have is the Lord's protection from day to day.

Death can come to us over a thousand ways, when we least expect it.

The only way that we can be protected is if the Lord protects us, because even in a split second we can get killed without the Lord's protection on any day.

The Lord's protection can also be meant for you and me to die for the Lord to save our souls from being lost in our sins so that we do not die the eternal death.

It can be profound to us that the only way that the Lord can protect someone's soul from being lost is to allow them to die, even at an early age, to protect their soul's salvation from eternal death.

This World

This world has nothing eternal to give to me.

This world only has temporary things to give to me.

As I live in this world from day to day, I only see things that can erode and rust and break down.

As I live in this world from day to day, I only see people who will one day die and go to the grave.

As I live in this world from day to day, I only see temporary things that will one day pass away.

This world has nothing eternal to offer me.

This world will only offer me temporary things that can surely let me down at any time in the day and night.

Only Jesus can give me eternal things because Jesus Christ is the eternal life beyond my temporary life that will fall very short for me and I might not live to see another day.

This world has nothing but temporary things in it, day after day, because of Adam and Eve disobeying God who created this world to be eternal from the very beginning.

Adam and Eve were eternal but they gave that up for a fruit that looked so good in their eyes but that fruit was filled with nothing but death.

This world has nothing eternal in it, and will one day pass away with every temporary thing in it.

Only Jesus Christ, our Lord and Savior, was without sin here on earth.

Jesus was the only eternal One who came from heaven to this world with the love of God for all the world.

This world has nothing eternal to give to anyone, but death will be eternal for the wicked who reject Jesus and live for the devil who is temporary to an eternal God in heaven.

The temporary things in this world will take away our eternal call from the Lord if we put temporary things before Him who had once lived and died in this world that could not keep Jesus in the grave.

The grave was only temporary to Jesus, who is the origin of life eternal forever beyond this world.

This world only has temporary things that can come and go like we never had anything in this world, just like the clothes we have on our backs that we didn't have on before we were born into this world.

This old sinful world is filled with only temporary things all around, and our days, weeks, months and years are so temporary to age us old to one day die.

This world has nothing eternal in it and time is surely proof of that because time will run out sooner or later in this world.

When that happens, our eternal Jesus Christ will come back again to eliminate time as if all who are saved in Jesus never experienced their time on earth.

That's because all who are saved in Jesus will become immortal because Jesus Christ gives eternal life to all the holy saints.

God's Holy Sanctuary

When we enter into God's holy sanctuary in the church, our minds should be meditated on the Lord so we can sit down quietly in the pews and wait for the song service to begin.

We should always reverence the Lord in His holy sanctuary and not be talking too much or moving around too much in church, especially on God's holy Sabbath day of rest.

We should not be busybodies on God's holy Sabbath day of rest; we need to respect the Lord Jesus Christ in His holy sanctuary where the Holy Spirit is very present, as are the holy angels who we can push out of the church if we make the church a social club on the holy Sabbath day of rest.

There's nothing wrong with talking to one another in God's holy sanctuary, as long as we don't talk too much.

There's nothing wrong with moving around in God's holy sanctuary, as long as we aren't moving around too much, because our attention needs to be on our Lord and Savior Jesus Christ when we are in God's holy sanctuary.

God's holy sanctuary is not a place where you and I need any distractions that could cause us to miss out on what the Sabbath school teacher is saying to us.

We need to be focused on the teachings to be blessed by the Lord.

If people are walking back and forth in God's holy sanctuary during the Sabbath school lesson hour, it will surely be distracting and we can miss out on something that even someone sitting down in the pews can say to enrich our relationship with the Lord.

It's always good to walk quietly in God's holy sanctuary because loud footsteps should not be heard there, especially during the Sabbath school lesson hour.

Only the Sabbath school teacher and those who participate in the Sabbath school lesson should be heard so that everyone can hear the sweet sound of the bible truth about the Lord Jesus Christ.

When the pastor is preaching a sermon in God's holy sanctuary, it is not the time to be moving around a lot and distracting people so that their minds are off of the Lord who is speaking through the pastor to encourage us all to love Him and keep His Commandments.

If a baby is crying during the sermon, the right thing to do is walk out of the sanctuary quietly with the baby so the service can continue for the church members and the visitors in the church to be blessed by the pastor's or elder's sermon uplifting the Lord's holy and wonderful name to all the congregation in the holy sanctuary, especially on God's holy Sabbath day of rest.

God's holy sanctuary is a very sacred place, whether it's in church on a Saturday or Sunday, because God has His true sheep in every church where we know what is right and don't do it, we sin against God.

There is supposed to be decency and order in God's holy sanctuary where the holy angels are also sitting down in the pews beside us to keep a record of our worship unto the Lord.

We can only worship in spirit and truth and not in moving around a lot and talking a lot in God's holy sanctuary.

All of the moving around a lot and talking a lot should be done outside of the holy sanctuary because it's never good to quench the Holy Spirit, especially in God's holy sanctuary where the Lord loves to show His strongest presence to give us the power to trample on serpents and scorpions and over all the power of the enemy so that nothing by any means can hurt us.

When we come together to worship and pray to the Lord in His holy sanctuary, we get more and more power from the Lord.

If we are moving around a lot and talking a lot in God's holy sanctuary, then we lose the power from the Lord because we're being busybodies in God's holy sanctuary.

Reverence unto the Lord in His holy sanctuary is the key to unlock God's heart to order our steps into His holy throne room where the devil can't enter and corrupt our worship unto the Lord.

Spiritually Overweight

Many people do see that they need to lose some weight off of their bodies and they will make a good effort to lose the weight.

There is another weight that many people don't see to lose and may not care to lose because they believe that other kind of weight looks good on them day after day.

Many people don't see that they need to lose the weight of gossip.

Many people don't see that they need to lose the weight of worry.

Many people don't see that they need to lose the weight of lust.

Many people don't see that they need to lose the weight of envy.

Many people don't see that they need to lose the weight of pride.

Many people don't see that they need to lose the weight of discontentment.

Many people don't see that they need to lose the weight of greed.

Many people don't see that they need to lose the weight of hatred.

Many people don't see that they need to lose the weight of strife.

Many people don't see that they need to lose the weight of covetousness.

Many people don't see that they need to lose the weight of manipulation.

Many people don't see that they need to lose the weight of selfishness.

Many people don't see that they need to lose the weight of telling lies.

Many people don't see that they need to lose the weight of murdering people.

Many people don't see that they need to lose the weight of stealing.

Many people don't see that they need to lose the weight of getting revenge.

Many people don't see that they need to lose the weight of holding grudges.

Many people don't see that they need to lose the weight of ruining people's lives.

It's so easy to see we're physically overweight, but it's hard to see when we're spiritually overweight if we don't read God's holy word that will show us how to lose those excessive pounds of sins that many people don't see and don't believe that they need to shed.

The only way to lose our spiritual weight is to confess and repent of our sins unto the Lord Jesus Christ, who is the only one who has the power to help us shed the spiritual weight without making us look like we are spiritually underweight because Jesus will not leave us spiritually malnourished.

There are many people who are not physically overweight, but they are spiritually overweight because they are living in their sins that they don't see and don't care to lose.

They believe they look so good and strut their sins wherever they go.

It's always good for us to lose the physical weight if we're overweight, because that will help us to look and feel better about ourselves.

It's much better to lose our excess spiritual weight that we surely need the Holy Spirit to help us to do, because it's easy to be spiritually overweight right in the church and believe we are in good spiritual health before the Lord.

The Lord can use someone who's not even in the church to let us know that we're spiritually overweight and it's crushing down on us because we are not living what we preach about Jesus.

It's much easier to lose our extra physical weight than it is to lose our extra spiritual weight because there will always be an excess of sin that we need to confess and repent of unto Jesus Christ who took on all of our spiritual weight of sins on the cross.

No matter how many pounds of fat we lose from our bodies so we can look so good and fit, Jesus truly sees how spiritually overweight we are even if we believe that we can run the spiritual race and endure to cross over the finish line.

Many people have already dropped out of the race because they're spiritually overweight.

People being spiritually overweight goes way back for thousands of years in the bible days when Cain was so spiritually overweight with envy that he killed his brother Abel because God accepted Abel's sacrifice and rejected Cain's sacrifice.

I am Calling on Jesus

While you are calling me a fake, I am calling on Jesus in my prayers and asking Him to forgive me of my sins, which is something you also need to do.

While you are calling me a phony, I am calling on Jesus in my prayers and asking Him to cleanse me of my sins, which you also need to do.

While you are calling me a hypocrite, I am calling on Jesus in my prayers and asking Him to help me to be real, which you also need to do.

While you are calling me a liar, I am calling on Jesus in my prayers and asking Him to help me to be true, which you also need to do.

While you are calling me a mental case, I am calling on Jesus in my prayers and asking Him to keep me in my right mind, which you also need to do.

While you are calling me a slow learner, I am calling on Jesus in my prayers and asking Him to enhance and sharpen my mind, which you also need to do.

While you are calling me stupid, I am calling on Jesus in my prayers and asking Him to give me wisdom, which you also need to do.

While you are calling me a weak link, I am calling on Jesus in my prayers and asking Him to give me strength, which you also need to do.

While you are calling me a peasant, I am calling on Jesus in my prayers and asking Him to bless me with spiritual wealth, which you also need to do.

While you are calling me every name but a child of God, I am calling on Jesus in my prayers and asking Him to help me to love Him and keep His Commandments, which you also need to do.

While you are calling me a devil, I am calling on Jesus in my prayers and asking Him to help me to be like Him, which you also need to do on your borrowed time from the Lord that could run out before my borrowed time from the Lord.

While you call me ignorant, I am calling on Jesus in my prayers and asking Him to give me His Holy Spirit to help me live by the truth of God's holy word and understand it so that I can also share it with others who believe in Jesus like me.

My spiritual level is never too low down for me to not call on Jesus in my prayers every day.

No One Can Handle God

No one can handle God, and we surely can't handle all of God's blessings.

There are people who believe that they can handle God and tell God what to do and what not to do.

King Pharaoh wanted to handle God by not letting God's people go after the first plague that King Pharaoh witnessed and believed he could handle God.

There are people who want to handle God, but they can't handle God's blessings.

It goes to their heads and they believe they made themselves prosperous.

God gives many people the ability to get a good education, which is a blessing from God that they can't handle because it goes to their heads and they start to believe they are so great.

Even in the church there are people who will let their spiritual gifts from God cause them to be proud and have no humility unto God.

There are church folks who believe they can handle God and make Him give them everything they pray and ask for.

They believe that God is supposed to give it to them because they believe they are worthy and right with God.

You and I must be careful what we pray for and believe we can handle it.

God truly always knows if we are ready to receive from Him what we ask for.

We all can want to handle God, but we can't handle all of His blessings as if we deserve to be blessed by God.

We can believe that God's Son, Jesus Christ, needs our favor upon Him to be the head of the church.

We can believe that we are the head of the church and can gather the wheat and throw out the tares in the church, when we can believe a wheat is a tare and a tare is a wheat.

No one can handle God, and surely not all of His blessings.

God can bless us with something great and it can go to our heads if we don't stay in prayer and ask the Lord to help us to keep pride from entering into our hearts.

It's so easy for us to believe that we can handle God's blessings.

God gives us life, health and strength that can go to our heads and make us believe that we are keeping ourselves alive and in good health and strength until we get ill.

All of the exercise and healthy foods have no power or control to keep us from getting sick.

It goes to show that we can't handle anything without God's Son, Jesus Christ, who Peter tried to handle when he took Jesus aside and began to rebuke him, saying, "Be it far from thee, Lord: This shall not be unto thee."

But Jesus turned to Peter and said, "Get thee behind me, Satan: thou are an offense unto me for thou savourest not the things that be of God, but those that be of men."

The Speed Limit of Life

Every road has a speed limit sign, whether you're driving on local roads, county roads or highway roads.

Every day so many drivers will drive over the speed limit as if there were no speed limit signs on the sides of the road.

Most drivers have driven over the speed limit at one time or another, especially drivers like you and me who have been driving for a long time and have gotten some speeding tickets.

So many people will drive over the speed limit as if they were driving a race car at the speedway where no speed limit signs exist.

When we drive over the speed limit, we break the law as if there is no law for drivers on the road.

An accident can easily happen when driving over the speed limit.

Many drivers have caused so many accidents on the roads because of driving over the speed limit as if they own the roads.

There is a speed limit of life that the Lord has given to all the world to keep His holy law that will never cause any spiritual accidents upon our souls.

There is a speed limit of life that has a speed limit sign called the Holy Bible that can keep us safe from spiritually driving down the road to hell that is filled with lawbreakers speeding to the dead-end road of eternal death for not living the truth of God's holy word that is the spiritual speed limit sign that points all in the world to Jesus Christ.

Jesus has given us the speed limit of life to abide by in this sinful world where so many accidents happen every day on the roads, mostly because of people driving over the speed limit.

The speed limit of life is trustworthy and every day it keeps us safe from that road-raging devil if we love and obey Jesus who is the only road to eternal life.

The only reason why many people will drive the speed limit is when they see a police car near by them.

So many people will ignore God's speed limit of life written in His holy word that is very near by them every day that they will speed up very fast on the wide and destructive roads of the devil.

The speed limit is for everybody's safety on the road.

There are a lot more spiritual accidents than physical accidents on the road, and it's the spiritual accidents that will surely bring eternal death upon anyone who doesn't obey the Lord's speed limit of life.

God's speed limit of life is for everybody's spiritual safety, but we have a free will to choose to obey the holy law of God that will not change when the speed limit on the roads can change.

It's So Easy to Believe

It's so easy to believe who we see and what we see from day to day, but it's hard for many people to believe what they can't see.

It's so easy for us to believe the sky is real, because we see the sky so very high above us.

It's so easy for me to believe that you are real, because I can see you.

It's so easy for you to believe that I am real, because you can see me.

It's so easy to believe who we see and what we see is real from day to day, but it's hard for many people to believe what they don't see.

It's so easy to believe that an animal is real, because we can see an animal.

It's so easy to believe that nature is real, because we can see nature.

It's so easy to believe that the sun is real, because we can see the sun shining.

It's so easy to believe that the dark night is real, because we can see the dark night.

It's so easy to believe who we see and what we see from day to day, but it's hard for many people to believe what they don't see.

It's so easy to believe the church that we see, but it's hard for many people to believe in an unseen Lord and Savior Jesus Christ, who they don't see.

It's so easy to believe the church that we see, but it's so hard for many people to believe in an unseen Lord and Savior Jesus Christ, who they don't see in many church-going folks.

It's so easy to believe that I am real and it's so easy for you to believe that you are real, because I can see me and you can see you from day to day.

It's so hard for many people to believe in an unseen Lord and Savior Jesus Christ.

It's so easy for every true child of God to believe in Jesus Christ, who we never see with our naked eyes, but it's so hard for even so-called Christians to believe in Jesus Christ because of their actions not being in line with God's holy word.

It's so easy to believe that who we see and what we see is real to us from day to day.

We don't need to question if who we see and what we see is real or not real to us.

The church building is real to many unbelievers who've never seen Jesus Christ who Christians go to church to worship.

An unbeliever has a very hard time believing in Jesus Christ, because they may question how we Christians should dress from day to day.

Every Christian is supposed to dress in modest apparel so unbelievers can see Jesus in us.

We aren't supposed to be attracting attention to ourselves.

We can talk all we want about Jesus, but if we know to do right by Jesus and don't do it, then we make it very hard for even spiritual babies in the church to believe in an unseen Lord and Savior Jesus Christ.

It's so easy to believe who we see and what we see from day to day, but we don't see Jesus Christ with our naked eyes.

We all can see the church buildings that were built by many men who don't believe in Jesus Christ, but will respect us Christians for believing in an unseen Lord and Savior Jesus Christ.

Jesus Never Promised Anyone

Jesus never promised anyone that they would join a church with perfect people, because the church is a spiritual hospital where sinners can be spiritually healed.

Jesus gave up His life on the cross to save every sinner from being lost in their sins.

That is what Jesus promised to us all, but He never promised anyone who repents and turns to Him that they would come into His church and never have any enemies.

Jesus never promised anyone that once we give our lives to Him our lives would be easy in the church.

Jesus lets us know that there would be tares that will pretend to be wheat in the church, and you and I can only pray that we are not a tare in the church.

Jesus never promised anyone that being a Christian would be easy, even in the church where cliques and favoritism can spread like a deadly virus.

Jesus never promised anyone that our spiritual gifts from Him would be a blessing to everyone in the church where there are folks who will get envious of you and me if they believe that we are out-shining them in the church.

Jesus never promised anyone who believes in Him that we would not go through any hardships for His holy name sake.

You and I can also go through some hardships in the church, where there are church folks who will play tricks on us spiritually, mentally, emotionally and psychologically and cause us to feel like we are lost right in the church.

Jesus never promised anyone that once we are saved in Him we are always saved in Him and can therefore spiritually abuse those who are weak in their faith and make them feel that their works are useless in the church because they don't have a college degree.

Jesus never promised anyone that everyone in the church would love them and rejoice with them when they are doing something great in Jesus' holy name.

There are church folks who will not love you and me and will not rejoice with us for doing something great in Jesus' holy name.

Jesus never promised anyone that the devil wouldn't come to church and would not be a leader in the church who tries to control our minds and make us believe that he or she is perfect and has no sins to confess and repent of unto the Lord Jesus Christ, who is the head of the church.

Jesus never promised anyone who denies self and picks up their cross and follows Him that their life would be full of red roses.

Even in the church red roses can dry up, wither away and leave the church because of so-called church folks being envious of especially red rose babes being on fire for Jesus in the church.

Jesus never promised anyone that they would not have to face up to death for His holy name's sake, but there are church folks who will act like going through a little trial for Jesus' name sake is killing them.

Jesus has promised to everyone that He will give us all eternal life for believing in Him who faced up to even eternal death on the cross when God turned His back on Jesus and he asked, "My God, why have You forsaken me?"

It was also like eternal life had forsaken Jesus to receive eternal death on the cross when Jesus became sin in our place to save us from our sins.

So-called Christians are keeping Jesus in the grave He rose from because they are spiritually dead in the church.

They mock you and me for trying our best to be real about loving Jesus and keeping His Commandments.

One of the reasons why many people leave the church is because they finally see through the so-called Christians who pretend to be like Jesus.

People can be so hurt by these so-called Christians, especially if they are going through some hard times in their lives and get no help from those they're very close to in the church.

Jesus never promised anyone that the devil will not appear as an angel of light in the church that only Jesus Christ is the head of to shake out anyone who is not like Him.

Jesus has his true remnant children in the church making no promises to new believers in Jesus that this Christian journey will be easy to be more and more like Jesus.

A One Day at a Time Journey

I must deny myself and pick up my cross and follow Jesus Christ one day at a time.

I can only choose to live my life unto the Lord one day at a time, and I can't skip over a day for the Lord not to see me making Him my choice or not making Him my choice.

I can only love Jesus one day at a time.

I can only pray to Jesus one day at a time.

I can only believe in Jesus one day at a time, that I can't speed up to go past Jesus.

Living my life unto Jesus Christ, my Lord, is a one day at a time journey, and I can't go anywhere beyond one day at a time.

God created the days in the beginning of His creation here on earth.

The Lord is so loving and fair to give you and me a one day at a time journey to spiritually walk down His road to be saved in Him one day at a time.

The Lord foreknew before He created this world that human beings wouldn't be able to keep up with His eternal fast pace.

Days don't exist in heaven, only here on earth, where the pace is slow for our one day at a time journey that the Lord foreknew to be good and right for you and me to keep up with.

You and I are only mortal beings and have a hard time getting through a one day at a time journey because even before the day comes to an end, you and I may be so exhausted and want to give up on something that we started our day off doing.

How can you and I ever understand that one thousand years is like one day to the Lord, who you and I can only love and obey one day at a time that we can only live in our bodies?

You and I can only deny ourselves and pick up our crosses and follow Jesus Christ, who will never lead us astray to be lost in our sins that Jesus gave up His life on the cross to save us from, one day at a time.

During Jesus last hours on the cross, He saved one of the thieves hanging on his cross because he made Jesus his choice on the last day that he lived one day at a time.

The thief made a wise choice beyond all of his past days that didn't matter to Jesus who knows that it takes one day at a time to make Him our choice, when it only takes one day to live for the devil and be lost in our sins.

A one day at a time journey is our only way to be saved in Jesus, because Judas was only pretending to be saved in Jesus but his deception showed and told on him the day that Judas betrayed Jesus.

Judas made up in his mind one day at a time that he would pretend to be one of Jesus' disciples, but only Jesus foreknew up in heaven beyond the days of Judas who Jesus knew to betray Him one day.

Jesus foreknew what Judas would do before Judas was ever born to live in this world only one day at a time.

If you and I have a hard time walking down the spiritual journey road to get closer and closer to Jesus, then how can anyone say that once they are saved they are always saved?

That would truly eliminate the hardships to go through that can only be one day at a time for Jesus' holy name sake.

Saying "Once I am saved, I am always saved" is truly saying that one day at a time doesn't exist at all for any Christian to pray and ask the Lord to forgive us of our sins.

That would mean there is no one day at a time that God gives us all a chance to repent.

We all have sins to fall short of the glory of God who is eternal and lives forever beyond our one day at a time journey that has no eternal time.

For anyone to believe that once they are saved they are always saved, is like saying "I have no sins to ever confess and repent of," which we can only do one day at a time on our journey to get closer and closer to Jesus.

Jesus will surely show us some new sins that we never saw as we get closer and closer to Him, which we can only do one day at a time on our Christian journey.

The Lord Will Not Let Us Off the Hook So Easily

When the Lord tells us to say something that we hold back and don't say, the Lord will not let us off the hook so easily until we say what He wants us to say.

When the Lord tells us to do something that we don't do, the Lord will not let us off the hook so easily until we do what He tells us to do.

The Lord didn't let Jonah off the hook so easily when Jonah didn't go down to Nineveh to tell the people to repent like the Lord told Jonah to do.

The Lord didn't let Jonah off the hook so easily because the Lord had commanded a whale to swallow Jonah down into its belly because Jonah disobeyed the Lord.

You and I should learn from Jonah's mistake that he made because of his selfish pride that caused Jonah to believe that those wicked people in Nineveh deserved to die in their sins.

When the Lord tells us to even write something and publish it in a book, if we don't do it then the Lord will not let us off the hook so easily until we write it and get it published in a book that the Lord knows someone will be truly blessed when he or she reads it.

The Lord will not let you and me off the hook so easily.

The Lord can easily hang us up on the hook of being guilty before Him and all the angels in heaven if we quench His Holy Spirit by putting off what the Lord tells us to say and do.

Two Different Voices that Speak to Us in Our Minds

Every day there are two different voices that speak to us in our minds and we can't do anything about it except pray to the Lord to help us to listen to and obey the right voice speaking in our minds.

There is a voice in our minds that will tell us to say something good.

There is a voice in our minds that will tell us to say something bad.

Two different voices can speak so kind to us in our minds.

There is a voice in our minds that will tell us to do something good

There is a voice in our minds that will tell us to do something bad.

Two different voices can speak to us so powerfully in our minds.

Sometimes, it can be hard for us to tell the difference between the two different voices that speak to us in our minds every day.

The two different voices will not give us a break to take for as long as we live, whether we're on our guard or off our guard.

The two different voices can speak to us in our minds for only you and me and the Lord God to hear those two different voices.

There is a voice in our minds that will tell us that we need to say this and say that.

There is a voice in our minds that will tell us that we need to do this and do that.

There is a voice in our minds that will tell us that we don't need to say this and say that.

There is a voice in our minds that will tell us that we don't need to do this and do that.

There is a voice in our minds that will tell us to wait before saying something.

There is a voice in our minds that will tell us to wait before we do something.

There is a voice in our minds that will tell us to say something right away.

Sometimes, it's hard for us to tell the difference between the right voice and the wrong voice that will speak to us in our minds in one way or in another way each and every day that many people are not in their right minds to be in tune with one's sanity.

We can be so thankful unto the Lord for giving us His holy word to let us know the difference between the two different voices that can speak to us in our minds.

We must read and meditate on God's holy word to help us to know the voice that is in line with every scripture in the holy bible that is the truth of God for us to live by every day.

If the word of God is not in our minds, then we won't know the difference between the two voices that can speak to us in our minds even when we are right there in church to show and tell by our actions which voice we listen to and obey.

We can listen to and obey the voice of the Holy Spirit speaking to us in our minds, or we can listen to and obey the voice of the devil speaking to us in our minds where the devil can also speak to us so kind and so convincingly in our minds.

Only the voice of God's Holy Spirit will always be in line with God's holy word that the Holy Spirit inspired the holy men of God to write for us to live by and voice our faith in Jesus Christ to all the world.

If we don't make a practice of reading God's holy word, then we won't be able to tell the difference between the two different voices that can speak to us in our minds for us to listen to and obey.

The voice we choose to listen to and obey will one way or another way be seen sooner or later in our actions, even in the church that the devil can also go to for the Lord to make him a defeated foe.

The two voices that speak to us in our minds today spoke to everyone back in the bible days when a few people out of millions of people listened to and obeyed the voice of the Holy Spirit telling them so kindly to fear God and keep His Commandments in their minds for their hearts to reveal their voices and actions being like Jesus.

Nothing in this World will Always Last

Nothing in this world will always last, just like money can come and money can go.

Nothing in this world will always last, just like a new house will one day get old.

Nothing in this world will always last, just like a new car will one day break down.

Nothing in this world will always last, just like new clothes will one day fade.

Nothing in this world will always last, just like new shoes will one day wear out.

Nothing in this world will always last, just like new furniture will one day get old.

Nothing in this world will always last, just like a new air conditioning unit will one day break down.

Nothing in this world will always last, just like a new TV will one day black out.

Nothing in this world will always last, just like a new job will one day take you into retirement.

Nothing in this world will always last, just like an animal can get old and die.

Nothing in this world will always last, just like you and I can get sick and die.

Nothing in this world will always last, just like you and I can age, get old and one day die.

Nothing in this world will always last, just like we can make friends and lose friends.

Nothing in this world will always last, just like we can get married and get a divorce.

Nothing in this world will always last, just like a mother can birth a baby and lose her baby.

Nothing in this world will always last, just like man and a woman and a boy and a girl can get rich and one day fall down into poverty.

Nothing in this world will always last, just like a water flood, wildfire, tornado, hurricane and earthquake can destroy everything that we have.

Nothing in this world will always last, because God's grace will one day close on this world.

Nothing in this world will always last, and the devil and his angels and his human agents will one day burn up in fire and brimstone.

Nothing in this world will always last, because even Jesus' church bride will one day leave this world and live with Him in heaven beyond this old world that has nothing in it that will always last.

We All are Human Beings

We all are human beings with one brain in our heads.

We all are human beings with two eyes to see.

We all are human beings with two ears to hear out of.

We all are human beings with one nose to breathe out of.

We all are human beings with one mouth to eat food and drink water.

We all are human beings with two arms to wrap around one another.

We all are human beings with two hands to pick up and hold something.

We all are human beings with two legs to stand up on.

We all are human beings with two feet to walk on.

We all are human beings with one body to live in.

We all are human beings, whether we are male or female.

We all are human beings who are meant to have all of our body parts, but every human being doesn't have all of his or her body parts.

There are human beings who were born without all of their body parts.

There are human beings that lose an arm or two or lose a leg or two in a war.

There are human beings who lose an eye or two or lose a hand or two in a war or in an accident.

Regardless of this, we all are still human beings created in the image of God, and so meant to be born with all of our body parts.

We all are human beings who the devil hates and will destroy.

The devil has already used many human beings to kill many other human beings, especially in a war.

The devil loves to turn human beings against one another, and he has been doing that for thousands of years.

The devil doesn't want to see any human being keeping God's ten Commandments of love.

The devil hates to see this.

We all are human beings who God loves so much that He gave us His only begotten Son that whosoever believeth in Him shall not perish but shall have eternal life.

The devil doesn't want to see any human being get all that he had when he once lived in heaven.

The devil doesn't want to see any human being choosing to repent and turn to Jesus Christ.

The devil knows that he will also burn in hell for the sins of every human being who will go back to heaven with Jesus when He comes back again on the clouds of glory.

We all are human beings who God wonderfully made in His image.

All of the fallen angels hate this and are trying their best to cause every human being to be lost in our sins like they are lost forever in their sins.

We all are human beings who God gave a free will to choose, and the devil hates this because he doesn't want to see you and me making Jesus our choice over him every day that we live.

We all are human beings who God created to worship Him who all the angels in heaven worship forever and ever, as well as all the unfallen worlds.

We all are human beings, whether we are male or female, who will answer to God for the choices that we make — whether they are good choices or bad choices.

We all are human beings who God will hold accountable for the right that we know to do but don't do it.

We all are human beings living in this world that Jesus Christ took back from the devil when He rose from the grave for no human being to have an excuse to believe that Jesus can't save any human being from their sins.

We all are human beings who can choose to believe in Jesus Christ and that He has dominion over this world that the first Adam lost for disobeying God who allowed the devil to have dominion over this world.

Jesus took back this world from the devil for every human being to be judged fairly in the courtroom of heaven where the devil can't appear to override Jesus' verdict of finding us innocent for being saved in Him who gives His saving grace to every human being.

We all are human beings who are vulnerable to the poisonous snake bite of death, no matter whether we're young, middle aged or old.

We all are human beings who need Jesus, whether we believe it or not.

We all are human beings who the devil wants to possess to do his evil, but we human beings can truly thank Jesus for becoming a human being like us with no sin in His flesh to show us the way that we were meant to be from the beginning of this world before Adam and Eve disobeyed God.

We all are human beings who can truly thank Jesus Christ for becoming a human being like us while He had no sins in His flesh to one day restore every human being back to the way that God created us in His perfect and glorious image.

We all are human beings who can truly thank Jesus Christ for becoming a human being like us, but only Jesus was without sin to make the devil a defeated foe against us human beings for choosing to believe in Jesus who can save the uttermost human being from being lost in sin.

Every human being can repent and turn to Jesus Christ before it's too late because Jesus gives every human being a chance to repent before we die.

We all are human beings and every human being who is in their right, mature mind will be held accountable by God for not living right by God when we know to live right by Him.

Jesus lived right by God when He lived in this world with no sin in His flesh, and he acted as every human being's right example, which the devil hates.

We all are human beings who can't pass by Jesus Christ and get to God and ask Him to accept us into heaven.

To get into heaven, we must believe in God's Son, Jesus Christ.

Many human beings don't believe that they must believe in Jesus Christ to be saved from their sins.

We all are human beings who God didn't waste His time to create in His image.

The devil has deceived many human beings into believing that all human beings are not created in the image of God because we are all different and have different skin complexions and different intellectual abilities.

We all are human beings, great and small, who can't blame God or the devil if we are lost in our sins because God has given all human beings a free will to choose.

The devil has no control over us and can't stop us from choosing to repent and turn to Jesus Christ before we die like the thief on the cross who chose to believe in Jesus Christ before he died on his cross.

We all are human beings living on the very edge of life in this sinful world where it's so easy to fall off the edge of righteous living and down into a sin that we can excuse as being a small thing.

God's grace is every human being's strong safety net to fall into with a chance to repent and turn to Jesus before the safety net of God's grace breaks on this whole world one day.

Only God knows when it's time for Jesus to stand up and say that it is finished, and every human being will remain righteous or wicked before God with nothing different in-between.

Lucifer Stopped Believing in God

Lucifer in all of his perfection and beauty stopped believing in God because he decided that he wanted to be God.

Lucifer believed that he was worthy to be God and that God was not worthy to be God.

Lucifer became the very first atheist up in heaven where he believed that God had no right to rule over him and he would not bow down and worship God.

Lucifer became so full of himself that he believed he could eliminate God and take God's place on His holy throne.

Lucifer wanted to be worshipped like God and he caused the other angels to become atheists with him up in heaven that God created and put the angels in heaven to worship Him.

Lucifer and one third of the angels in heaven stopped believing in God.

Michael the archangel commanded his angels to fight against Lucifer and his angels up in heaven.

Lucifer and his angels lost that war and were cast out of heaven, along with their atheist idea that there is no God to rule over them in heaven.

God could have spoken one word to eliminate Lucifer and his angels as if they never existed in heaven, but God was very fair to two thirds of His angels and let them be in on the war to prove their love for God to the rebellious angels.

Lucifer, in all his perfection, stopped believing in God.

So, who are we professed Christians to believe that we can't do the same thing Lucifer did up in heaven?

When it comes to losing a very dear loved one, especially at a very young age, our faith in the Lord will truly be tested.

At this time, we will have to choose whether we're going to stop believing in Jesus Christ or if we're going to continue to believe in Him and not question Him or get angry at Him for allowing our very dear loved one to die at a very young age.

There are many different ways for any Christian to stop believing in Jesus Christ, the Son of God.

We can choose to keep our belief in Jesus Christ, no matter what hardships come along to weigh us down, because we know Jesus will give us the strength to bear our burdens because we've put all of our trust in Him.

Lucifer and one third of the angels in heaven stopped believing in God, who created them to worship Him forever and ever.

It's the same thing for you and me to worship God's Son, Jesus Christ, forever and ever in heaven, if we make it there, because only Jesus can take us there when He comes back again on the clouds of glory.

When Lucifer stopped believing in God, it was not a big surprise to God who knows all things and knows what we will think before we think it, say before we say it and do before we do it.

God created the angels with a free will to choose, because God is love and will not control us.

God will not control the angels and He will not control you and me or force us to believe in Him.

Anyone who stops believing in God's Son, Jesus Christ, will only cause themselves the greatest loss that would mean they'd be better off to have never been born.

It's much better to never believe in Jesus than to have once believed in Jesus and turned your back on Him.

Doing this would make you and me more worse off than any atheist.

At least an atheist has more dignity about believing there is no God than anyone who once believed in God and then turned their back on God for whatever reason.

Doing this is senseless to even the birds that can sense that there is a true, living God who feeds them day after day.

The Prison Door of Sin

Jesus unlocked the prison door of sin when He died on the cross and rose from the grave to destroy all of the devil's locks so that everyone could walk out of his prison cells.

No one can believe that they are locked up in the devil's prison, because they choose to stay in the devil's prison by living in their sins.

Jesus unlocked the prison door of sin, but many people are so deceived by the devil that they believe his prison door of sin is still locked and they cannot be set free.

Jesus unlocked the prison door of sin, but many people just don't want to let go of their sins and repent so they can walk out of the devil's prison and walk towards Jesus.

Jesus is the living, golden key that will unlock every prison door of sin so that anyone can walk out of the devil's notorious prison.

We can walk out of that prison because Jesus will not allow the devil to have any control over our free will choice to believe in Him.

The locks on the prison doors of sin have been broken by our Lord and Savior Jesus Christ, who will one day lock the devil up in the prison of a burning hell along with his fallen angels and human agents.

Jesus Christ, our Lord, unlocked the prison door of sin, but many people will refuse to open the door and walk out because they cannot believe that Jesus will unlock the prison door of sin for them if they make the choice to repent and turn to Him.

Jesus is the Only Way to Heaven

You can't preach your way to heaven.

You can't prophet your way to heaven.

You can't teach your way to heaven.

Jesus is the only way to heaven.

You can't pray your way to heaven.

You can't sing your way to heaven.

You can't diet your way to heaven.

Jesus is the only way to heaven.

You can't organize your way to heaven.

You can't administrate your way to heaven.

You can't talk your way to heaven.

Jesus is the only way to heaven.

You can't mission your way to heaven.

You can't fly your way to heaven.

You can't pilot your way to heaven.

Jesus is the only way to heaven.

You can't write your way to heaven.

You can't educate your way to heaven.

You can't witness your way to heaven.

Jesus is the only way to heaven.

You can't evangelize your way to heaven.

You can't service your way to heaven.

You can't smile your way to heaven.

Jesus is the only way to heaven.

You can't reason your way to heaven.

You can't opinionate your way to heaven.

You can't tithe your way to heaven.

Jesus is the only way to heaven.

You can't heal your way to heaven.

You can't study your way to heaven.

You can't work your way to heaven.

Jesus is the only way to heaven, which Jesus created.

We must believe in Jesus Christ to be saved and enter into heaven when Jesus comes back again on the clouds of glory.

You can't earn your way to heaven.

You can't beautify your way to heaven.

You can't modest apparel your way to heaven.

Jesus is the only way to heaven.

You can't temperance your way to heaven.

You can't wellness your way to heaven.

You can't correct your way to heaven.

Jesus is the only way to heaven.

You can't prosper your way to heaven.

You can't minister your way to heaven.

You can't dream your way to heaven.

Jesus is the only way to heaven.

You can't righteous your way to heaven.

You can't win your way to heaven.

Jesus is the only way to heaven.

You can't plan your way to heaven.

You can't theory your way to heaven.

You can't scholar your way to heaven.

Jesus is the only way to heaven.

You can't dance your way to heaven.

You can't genius your way to heaven.

You can't award your way to heaven.

Jesus is the only way to heaven.

You can't favor your way to heaven.

You can't testimony your way to heaven.

Jesus is the only way to heaven.

You can't entertain your way to heaven.

You can't transparent your way to heaven.

You can't bold your way to heaven.

Jesus is the only way to heaven.

You can't confident your way to heaven.

You can't humble your way to heaven.

You can't explore your way to heaven.

Jesus is the only way to heaven.

You can't engineer your way to heaven.

You can't technician your way to heaven.

You can't navigate your way to heaven.

Jesus is the only way to heaven.

You can't hygiene your way to heaven.

You can't technology your way to heaven.

You can't romance your way to heaven.

Jesus is the only way to heaven because Jesus is the creator of all existence through His self-existence with God the Father and the Holy Spirit.

You can't marry your way to heaven.

You can't singleness your way to heaven.

You can't govern your way to heaven.

Jesus Christ, our Lord and Savior, is the only way for anyone to make it to heaven for believing in Him.

Love

Love can put a big smile on our face.

Love can put a spring in our step.

Love can give us a good night's sleep.

Love can take our worry away.

Love can save our life.

Love can relieve us of our stress.

Love can take away our doubt.

Love can take away our fears.

Love can give health to our body.

Love can ease our mind.

Love can heal our broken heart.

Love can encourage us to wise up.

Love can dry up our tears.

Love can give us the strength to keep going on.

Love can encourage us to be honest with ourselves.

Love can give us hope.

Love can prolong our life.

Love can make us sure about accepting one another for who we are.

Love can build us up when we are broken down.

Love can give health to our mind.

Love can clear up our mind from confusion.

Love can encourage us to be honest with others who are dishonest.

Love can be trusted.

Love cannot fail us.

Love can encourage us to use our bad experiences in life to help strengthen others who are weak.

Love can encourage us to do the right thing.

Love can encourage us to be real with one another.

Love can encourage us to believe in Jesus Christ, who is the love of God.

Love can encourage us to be patient with one another.

Love can help us to keep our sanity.

Love can encourage us to treat one another right.

Love can give us justice.

Love can encourage us to forgive one another.

Love can help us to find out the truth.

Love can encourage us to keep God's Commandments of love for Him and one another.

Love can encourage us to humble ourselves unto the Lord.

Love can encourage us to help those who are less fortunate than we are.

Love can help us to treat our pets right.

Love can help us to treat ourselves right.

Love cannot break God's Commandments.

Love cannot lose faith in Jesus Christ.

Love cannot believe that there is no God who is love.

Love cannot make us turn our back on Jesus Christ.

Love cannot reject Jesus Christ.

Love cannot lie to you and me.

Love cannot hurt you and me.

Love cannot deceive you and me.

Love can find us if we are lost in our sins.

Love can encourage us to make good choices in our life.

Love can lead us to Mount Calvary for us to know without a doubt that God so loved the world that He gave us His only begotten Son that whosoever believeth in Him shall not perish but shall have eternal life.

Love will one day cause all the saints to judge the fallen angels and all who are lost in their sins.

All of the saints in heaven will know that God is right to cast the wicked into hell.

All who make it to heaven will know that God is very fair in letting them judge the wicked who rejected Jesus who is the greatest love of God forever and ever.

Obey God

The universe has to obey God to keep all the stars and planets in its infinite vastness.

Black holes in the outer space have to obey God and not suck up the planets.

The stars obey God and shine in the outer space.

The moon has to obey God and circles the planet.

The planets obey God and circle around the sun.

The sky has to obey God and hover over the Earth.

The gravity has to obey God and to keep us on the ground so we don't float up into the outer space.

The day has to obey God to energize us.

The night has to obey God to relax us so we can get some sleep.

Nature has to obey God and give us its tranquility.

The animals obey God and don't form an army to go to war with us.

The air has to obey God to give us breath to breathe.

Time has to obey God and give us its borrowed time so we can be saved in Jesus Christ before it's too late.

Grace has to obey God and won't close on this world before everybody hears the gospel of Jesus Christ.

Chance has to obey God to give everybody a chance to repent and turn to Jesus.

Only you and I can be stubborn enough to disobey God, even in ways that we don't see and can believe we are right to hold onto one sinful thought that God hates.

One day soon, sin will obey God and bow down before God, knowing that God is right to burn up all sin in the lake of fire.

A Moment in Time

God gives us all a moment in time.

We can choose to live our moment in time unto the Lord Jesus Christ or unto the devil.

We are born into this world and very many of us go through the process of growing up into an adult in our moment in time.

We just don't always understand why God doesn't allow many children and teenagers to reach adulthood in their moment in time during this life on earth.

Everyone who knows to do right and doesn't do right in their moment in time that God give to them causes their moment in time to believe that they were better off never to have been born.

We were all born into this world to believe in Jesus Christ every day that God gives us life so we can live it unto the Lord Jesus Christ in our moment in time under the sun.

Time is limited for you and me and we will one day return to the dust.

Only the righteous living and the living wicked people will have their moment in time that will be left for them to be alive on earth in only a moment before Jesus comes back again on the clouds of glory with all the angels in heaven with Him.

In their very moment in time, the righteous living will be sealed in Jesus Christ and will not drop dead when they see Jesus in the brightness of His eternal power and glory on the clouds of glory.

In their very moment in time, the living wicked people will drop dead when they see Jesus in the brightness of His eternal power and glory on the clouds of glory.

Even before Jesus raises the righteous dead out of their graves, the righteous living will have their moment in time to cry out their hope with all of their breath unto the Lord as they look up and see a dark figure the size of a man's hand appearing to them up in the sky before Jesus brightens the sky with His power and glory.

Jesus will raise the righteous dead before he changes the righteous living from mortal to immortality in the twinkling of an eye.

God gives everyone their moment in time for His purpose that even we Christians can't always know, especially like Job who lost all of his children and all of his cattle in his moment in time when Job also became very ill to serve God's purpose.

God gives us all a moment in time that is all about doing God's will and not our own will which can shorten our lives in our moment in time.

God gives us all a moment in time under the sun where our time is short-lived below the unlimited eternal life in Jesus Christ, who time bows down unto and worships.

If We Pray and Ask the Lord for Wisdom

If we pray and ask the Lord for wisdom, He will give us the wisdom to do the right thing.

If we pray and ask the Lord for wisdom, He will give us the wisdom to say the right words

One day, in the morning about halfway to the noon hour, a man knocked lightly on my front door while I was sitting down in my living room resting along with my two little dogs.

My two little dogs didn't hear the knock on the front door.

I got up out of my chair and walked to the door.

I opened the front door and a man asked me, "Do you have Direct TV service in your home?"

I said yes, and right after I said that, he asked, "Is your Direct TV bill more than one hundred dollars?"

Then he asked if I had a black box with a model number on it.

I told him I had two black boxes, one upstairs and one downstairs on my TVs.

He then told me the names of other people who had Direct TV, and I asked if they lived in my same area.

He asked me again if my Direct TV cable bill was over one hundred dollars.

I told him, "No, my bill is only $67."

Hearing that, he told me I was all right.

I truly thank the Lord for giving me the wisdom to not let him come into my house and get the model number off my Direct TV black box.

I just don't know if he was honest with me or if he was being dishonest about being from the Direct TV company.

During the whole time I talked with him, I only opened the front door a little bit because I didn't see a Direct TV service vehicle in the parking lot where I live.

Because of this and all of his odd questions, I was cautious.

The Lord gave me some wisdom that sunny morning while the devil didn't care if I was well or sick, happy or sad because the devil is all about causing you and me to make foolish choices.

If we pray and ask the Lord for wisdom, He will give us the wisdom to not say or do something that the devil and his human agents will try to scam us into saying and doing.

My knowledge about my Direct TV service was not enough to keep me from letting the man come into my house to look at the model number on my Direct TV black box.

It was truly the wisdom the Lord gave to me to be more than enough of doing the right thing because with my Direct TV knowledge I had, I still could have made the wrong choice and let him talk me into letting him come into my house to get the model number.

Had I done that, it could have been my regret.

It's always good to have knowledge about what we need to know, but wisdom from the Lord will truly keep us safe from trouble that an educated fool can surely believe to be safe to walk into and hang around.

The Lord revealed to me that many people who have Direct TV are paying over a hundred dollars a month because they have a lot of channels on their TV, but it could be a scam that the man is using to cause people to believe they are paying a lot more money than what they are supposed to pay on their Direct TV bill.

He might have been using this to get his foot in the door of their house to get the model number off their Direct TV black box to use for his deceptive purpose.

Wisdom from the Lord sees right through deception that is powerful enough to spiritually blind an educated man and woman and lead them into foolishness.

This can also happen in the church, where everyone doesn't pray and ask the Lord for wisdom to show and tell in their words and actions.

You and I need to pray and ask the Lord for wisdom every day, because it doesn't take much effort to say and do something foolish that is surely not like the Lord Jesus Christ, who we Christians are supposed to be like before one another and unbelievers day after day.

Jesus is all-wise and has plenty of His wisdom to give to you and me if we only ask Him to give it to us.

This wisdom is beyond the bible knowledge that we have.

Only the wisdom of the Lord can protect us from saying and doing things we shouldn't say and do.

The Holy Spirit

The Holy Spirit won't tell us to tell a lie, but the devil will tell us to lie.

The Holy Spirit won't puff us up with pride, but the devil will puff up our pride.

The Holy Spirit won't tell us to get revenge, but the devil will tell us to get revenge.

The Holy Spirit won't tell us to not forgive those who do us wrong, but the devil will tell us to never forgive those who do us wrong.

The Holy Spirit won't tell us to cheat on our spouse, but the devil will tell us to cheat.

The Holy Spirit won't tell us to kill someone, but the devil will tell us to kill.

The Holy Spirit won't tell us to do bad things, but the devil will always tell us to do bad things.

The Holy Spirit won't tell us to steal, but the devil will definitely tell us to steal.

The Holy Spirit won't tell us to disobey our parents when they tell us what is good and right for us, but the devil will tell us to disobey our parents.

The Holy Spirit won't tell us to not return a faithful tithe and offering, but the devil will tell us not to return tithes and offerings faithfully.

The Holy Spirit won't tell us a lie, but all the devil does is tell us lies.

The Holy Spirit will tell us that the bible is all the truth for us to live by, but the devil will tell us the bible is a fairy tale book that only weak-minded people live by, when believing in Jesus Christ will make anyone's mind as strong as steel..

God is in Nature

God is in nature but God is not in our sinful nature that has immoral disasters of lies that can spread like a wild fire.

God is in nature but God is not in our sinful nature that has immoral disasters of selfishness that can be like a hurricane.

God is in nature but God is not in our sinful nature that has immoral disasters of pretense that can be like a drought.

God is in nature but God is not in our sinful nature that has immoral disasters of pride that can be like a raging flood.

God is in nature but God is not in our sinful nature that has immoral disasters of lust that can be like a mudslide.

God is in nature but God is not in our sinful nature that has immoral disasters of favoritism that can be like a sinkhole.

God is in nature but God is not in our sinful nature that has immoral disasters of envy that can be like an earthquake.

God is in nature but God is not in our sinful nature that has immoral disasters of revenge that can be like a famine.

God is in nature but God is not in our sinful nature that has immoral disasters of grudges that can be like a tornado.

God is in nature but God is not in our sinful nature that has immoral disasters of deceptions that are like a heatwave.

God is in nature but God is not in our sinful nature that has immoral disasters of discontent that can be like a snow blizzard.

We can surely see that natural disasters are very bad, but we often tend to overlook our sinful nature being worse than any natural disaster.

The sinful nature has killed more people than any natural disaster that will never be more deadly than immoral disasters caused by the sinful nature.

We all can thank God for giving us His Son, Jesus Christ, to save us from our sins.

It was the sins of Adam and Eve that caused this world to have natural disasters springing up from the root of Adam and Eve's immoral disaster of disobeying God.

God is in nature every day, and nature is beautiful and peaceful all around the world, but the sinful nature is very unattractive and troublesome to God every day.

The Power of Truth

When someone tells you the truth, you feel the power of the truth all through your mind and heart.

Everyone who loves to tell the truth will feel the power of the truth from the tip of their tongues.

Everyone who loves to hear the truth will feel the power of the truth sounding so good in their ears.

Everyone who loves to see the truth will feel the power of the truth looking so convincing to them in their eyes.

Everyone who loves to live the truth will feel the power of the truth in their life every day they live.

Even many liars will feel the power of the truth making them feel guilty for not telling the truth.

The power of the truth will always be in God's holy word to cause sinners like me and you to feel convicted of our sins so that we want to repent and turn to Jesus one day at a time because once we are saved doesn't mean that we are always saved in Jesus.

The power of the truth is a one day at a time power for us to feel the truth of, especially the word of God penetrating in our minds and hearts to power us up to live right unto the Lord.

The power of the truth originates from our Lord and Savior, Jesus Christ, who is the everlasting truth forever beyond the devil's lies that are only temporary and will be destroyed in the lake of fire where all the wicked won't have any power to escape God's great wrath upon them.

All who love the truth of God's holy word will feel the power of the truth setting them free from the false beliefs in this sinful world where lies can pretend to be truth.

There is nothing else in this world that can power up our minds and hearts more than the truth of God's holy word that is all truth about

God who so loved the world that He gave us His only begotten Son so that whosoever believeth in Him shall not perish but shall have eternal life.

The power of the truth is eternal in Jesus Christ who is the word of God, when death is like only one little typo in only one book out of millions of books.

That one little typo called death will be corrected when Jesus comes back again with every name written in His book of life that has no typos.

All of the angels will see that great number in the book that only Jesus can count to go back with Him to heaven.

That is the power of the everlasting truth of God.

That Will be Eternal, Except

There is nothing in this fallen world that will be eternal, except all who are saved in Jesus who will make all of the saints eternal one day in heaven.

When He comes back again to call all of His righteous dead out of the grave, that will be no prank to play on the righteous dead.

There is nothing in this fallen world that will be eternal one day, except the righteous living, who Jesus will change from mortal to immortality in the twinkling of an eye, which will cause the devil to curl up in the womb of the world that will be filled with the darkness of sin.

All who are lost in their sins will pass away in the dust of death for a thousand years.

There is nothing in this fallen world that will be eternal one day, except all the righteous not being left behind in this temporary world where the breath of the wicked dead will only reappear in the second resurrection to melt in fire and brimstone.

We just don't know if Jesus will make the animals and the reptiles and the birds and insects in this fallen world be eternal one day in heaven for us to see our pets being immortal in the heavenly land where everything is eternal up in heaven right now to never pass away.

There is Only One Afterlife

There is only one afterlife that is in Jesus Christ and not in Buddha, Hindu and Mohammad, whose lives are over in the grave that Jesus got the victory over when He rose from the grave.

Enoch, Moses and Elijah received that afterlife in Jesus Christ, who created the worlds and all things seen and unseen, whether they are great or small.

When Jesus rose from the grave there were many holy people who rose with Him and they walked through the Jerusalem holy city for people to know that they will live in the afterlife with Jesus who took them all back with Him to heaven because they were His precious gems.

There is only one afterlife that is in Jesus Christ and not in luck, magic, science, astronomy or technology that a trillion bucks can buy and sell to the very rich fools who don't believe in Jesus Christ to be the Son of God who has eternal wealth that you and I will truly see in the afterlife.

There is no afterlife in any animal or material thing — those are temporary under the sky where there is no afterlife in the seen things that are not eternal and will not give you and me the afterlife.

There is only one afterlife and that is in Jesus Christ, not any angel or bishop, pastor or pope who has sins and will one day die.

No one can raise themselves from the dead — that is the end of the living.

The only ones who will live on in the afterlife are those who believe in Jesus Christ.

Jesus Is

As the sun rises, Jesus is the King of kings and Lord of lords.

As the sun sets, Jesus is our rest, especially on His holy Sabbath day of rest.

As the stars sparkle, Jesus is the lily in the valley.

As the moonlight glows, Jesus is the wonderful counselor.

As the ocean waves splash, Jesus is the Almighty God.

As the river water flows, Jesus is "I am that I am."

As the earth rotates on its axis, Jesus is the creator of all things.

As the stars fall, Jesus is the Greatest of the great.

As the wind blows, Jesus is the way to go.

As the rain falls, Jesus is our All and all.

As the clouds form up in the sky, Jesus is the life to live.

As the shadows move across the landscape, Jesus is real.

As the earth shakes, Jesus is our solid rock.

As the grass dries up, Jesus is living waters.

As the mountain reaches up to its peak, Jesus is in heaven on high.

As we live our life, Jesus is the everlasting life.

As the earth groans in pain, Jesus is the healer of healers.

As time seems like only a moment, Jesus is forever present.

As the black holes appear in the outer space, Jesus is the bright and morning star.

As the devil roars like a lion, Jesus is the lion of Judah.

As the devil tempts us, Jesus is our victory.

As this world will one day pass away, Jesus is the beginning and the end.

As a fool says that there is no God, Jesus is the Son of God.

As we live and one day die, Jesus overcame the world to give us eternal life for believing in Him.

As the unfallen worlds keep a distance forever away from this world, Jesus is one with God and the Holy Spirit to never distance apart from their self-existence in the presence of all the worlds that Jesus created for the glory of the trinity Godhead.

Jesus is the Lamb of God

Jesus is the Lamb of God who shed His blood on the cross to pay our sinful cost, which no animal sacrifice could ever do since way back to the fall of Adam and Eve in the Garden of Eden that they had to leave out of with their sins.

Jesus is the one and only holy Lamb of God who put an end to all the animal sacrifices for you and me to come to Him to cleanse us of our sins and set us free from living in sin that Jesus Christ became on the cross for eternal life to stand still and not move one inch away from the ancient of days.

The holy and precious Lamb of God is Jesus Christ who said to Moses, "I am that I am" from the burning bush.

Jesus is the ultimate Lamb of God who won't push anyone into making Him our first choice over the temporary things in this lost world where only Jesus can save us if we believe in Him who will come back again on the clouds of glory one day to take us to heaven for being saved in Him today.

Tomorrow might be too late to repent and turn to Jesus who gave us all a free will to choose our fate in the maturity of our minds that a little child doesn't have to choose one's fate that God will do so meek and mild.

The Master of its

The sun is the master of its light
all day long that the sun will shine bright.

The moon is the master of its glow
all night long wherever we go.

The stars are the master of its sparkle
all night long that we can marvel at the stars no matter where we are.

The ocean is the master of its waves
that surfers will greatly embrace to ride on every day.

The river is the master of its flow
whether the flow is fast or slow.

The sky is the master of its atmosphere
whether the sky is cloudy or clear.

The mountain is the master of its cliff
no matter who climbs to the top of it with or without full gear.

Death is the master of the grave
but Jesus Christ is the master of life to save us from being lost in our
sins
before our life ends.

Jesus Christ is the master of victory for us to win
the prize of eternal life for believing in Him.

The strait and narrow road is the master of a slim chance
for the righteous to be saved over the rim of hell.

The devil is the master of the wicked
to be lost with no chance to even glance upon making it
to the heavenly, incorrupt, eternal land.

Who is Man?

Who is man to be like a bubble that bursts in thin air wherever he goes, here and there?

Who is man to be like a lightbulb that blows out at any time that we don't know to calculate under the sunshine?

Who is man to have control over his life that death can invade and take control over his breath?

Who is man to be here today and gone today down in the deep pit of death to return to the dust on the ground?

Who is man to be broken like glass by the uncertainty that can close its curtains on man's stage of life?

No man can put on a show before God and receive applause.

Who is man to be something without Jesus Christ who knitted him together in his mother's womb where he was nothing and could make no right or wrong choices in his fetal life?

Who is man that God created a woman for, to hold her as his most precious gem in one flesh of marital matrimony?

A man with another man and a woman with another woman can't band together in the presence of God and expect to get His approval of their marriage in a land where sin came upon all creatures from a man.

Who is man to put trust in day after day?

A man is a fool to put trust in himself, no matter where he lives, doing that would prove he is a fool to put his trust in anything in this world that could not pay our price on cross for our sins.

Jesus paid that cost with His life for every man, woman, boy and girl.

We can put all of our trust in Jesus Christ, who trust begins in and ends in day after day because Jesus is our best friend.

Everybody Who Ever Lived

Everybody who ever lived in this world had their chance to love and obey God in their day in time down through the ages of their days here on earth.

This is true all the way back to Adam and Eve, who were the first human beings on earth.

Adam and Eve had their chance to believe what God told them about not eating that fruit from the tree of knowledge and good and evil, but they disobeyed God and were shut out of the Garden of Eden and had to go maybe live in a hut.

Everybody who ever lived had their chance to love and obey God during their lifetimes before going down in the grave.

Everybody who is alive today has their chance to love and obey God in their right, mature minds and to understand that God gave us His only begotten Son, Jesus Christ, to save us from our sins and redeem us back to Him through the price Jesus paid with His life on the cross.

Everybody who ever lived in their right, mature mind from the north to the south and from the east to the west side of this world had their chance to choose to detest sin and love and obey God, who detests sin but loves every soul to be saved in His Son, Jesus Christ, who was foretold in the bible by the prophets of old speaking the truth to everybody in love to set them free from the devil's lies about God.

The devil is still telling lies about God before everybody who is alive today.

Everybody in their right, mature mind has a chance to love and obey God, and we need to choose to do this before it's too late.

No one has an excuse to say that God didn't give them a chance to love and obey Him as they lived in their right, mature minds, knowing right from wrong because God revealed this to all humanity in His holy law that Jesus came to this world to fulfill.

O Lord, All of Your Blessings are Great

O Lord, all of Your blessings are great and not small.

It's a great blessing to have eyes to see.

It's a great blessing to have ears to hear.

It's a great blessing to have a mouth to talk, eat food and drink water with.

It's a great blessing to have hands to hold anything.

It's a great blessing to have arms to hug with, especially our loved ones.

It's a great blessing to have legs to stand on.

It's a great blessing to have feet to walk on.

O Lord, all of Your blessings are great and not small.

O Lord, many people will take Your great blessings to be something small to them, until they lose their eyesight.

O Lord, many people will take Your great blessings to be something small to them, until they lose their hearing.

O Lord, many people will take Your great blessings to be something small to them, until they lose their voice.

O Lord, many people will take Your great blessings to be something small to them, until they lose a hand or two.

O Lord, many people will take Your great blessings to be something small to them, until they lose an arm or two.

O Lord, many people will take Your great blessings to be something small to them, until they lose a foot or two.

O Lord, all of Your blessings are great and not small.

O Lord, many people will take Your great blessings to be something small to them, until they are on their sick bed and might be dying.

O Lord, it's a great blessing from You to be alive and well.

O Lord, many people will take Your great blessings to be something small to them, until they lose their minds.

All of Your blessings are great and not small, my Lord and Savior Jesus Christ who created the heavens to be a great place to live in forever and ever.

O Lord, You created this world to be a great place to live in before Adam and Eve ate that fruit from the tree of knowledge, good and evil that was in the midst of the Garden of Eden.

O Lord, all of Your blessings are great and not small.

Many people, even in the church, will carry themselves like they are self-made, when it was You who made them prosperous through Your great blessings upon them.

O Lord, all of Your blessings are great to me who didn't bring myself this far in my life.

You did that for me, O Lord, when I deserve to be six feet down in the ground.

O Lord, many people will take Your great blessings to be something small until they lose everything they have.

Even then, they still may not see that all they had was from You giving them Your great blessings, because anything they had and now have belongs to You, O Lord.

No One is Worthy

No one is worthy of the Lord Jesus Christ's call to repent and turn to Him before it's too late.

There are people in the church who believe that they are God sent and worthy of the Lord's call radiating through the gates of heaven and down on all of those who will humble themselves before the Lord.

No one is worthy of the Lord's call because we all were born in the pagan of sin that the Lord called Abraham out of, and not because he was worthy to be called out of a pagan nation.

Many are called but a few are chosen, and not because they are worthy to be chosen by the Lord who will blot out anyone's sins if we confess and repent that the Lord calls everyone to do because everyone is not worthy of the Lord's call under the sun.

Everyone has a free will to choose to live for the Lord who shown no respect of persons to be chosen by Him.

There are church folks who are so sure of themselves and think they're so worthy of the Lord's call below the heavens .

We are chosen by the Lord and poke holes in the devil's lies.

No one is worthy of the Lord's call to be chosen under the sky.

You and I can be chosen by the Lord and still can be prone to deceive ourselves and think we're more worthy than those who we believe were not called by the Lord whose almighty hand can reach way down in sin and pull up the uttermost sinner who God loves to be His chosen.

No one in the church and outside the church is worthy to be chosen by the Lord, because we are all messed up sinners who can't save ourselves even in our new spiritual birth.

You and I can be spiritually ill in the church for the Lord to detest and not make us His chosen no matter how much we give Him our all.

Our all doesn't even come anywhere close to a small thing before an almighty, holy and righteous eternal God who no one is worthy to even speak His holy and eternal name.

The Most Beautiful Woman in this World

The most beautiful woman in this world is the church, which will one day walk with Jesus through the gates of pearls.

O what a very beautiful woman with the most beautiful eyes watching over every soul from coast to coast all around the world.

She is filled with the Holy Ghost, regardless of the tares that are no match to her as she boasts about her husband, Jesus Christ, who no one can match up to.

O what beautiful hands she has to hold up those who are weak in their faith wherever they go from day to day.

She holds onto Jesus Christ who keeps her strong and lets her get a good grip on anyone's life to repent and turn to God.

O what beautiful lips she has to speak the name of Jesus, even to the people living the street life that she invites into the church.

She shows no respect of persons to put to work for Jesus, no matter how bad life has beaten someone up and hurt their heart with a cheap low blow below the belt of life.

O what beautiful feet she has to walk the extra mile with anyone who knows that her talk and walk go together every day and every night in a sinner's eyesight so they have no excuse to not make the right choice to deny self and pick up their cross and follow Jesus Christ.

The most beautiful woman in this world is the church that will never age or grow old, and her beauty will never fade away from Jesus who loves her forever and ever.

In the Fullness of Time

Jesus came to this world in the fullness of time to set the pace for all human beings to be saved in Him in these last days.

Jesus came to this world in the fullness of time for no one to be left behind to be lost in their sins.

Today, no one in their right mind has an excuse to say that it's not their time to repent and turn to Jesus who is so divine to save everyone who believes in Him.

In our moment in time in this world, time was originated for you and me who were born in sin.

Jesus came to this world in the fullness of time that the devil hates because Jesus set the time clock of eternity to wake us up from our spiritual sleep so we can see that God is always an on-time God to give us His goodness that leads us to repent.

It is up to us to repent, which we can choose to do no matter how many odds are up against us during our time on earth where God sent His only begotten son to save us from our sins.

Jesus came to this world in the fullness of time that the devil can't turn back to pull us down like crabs in a barrel.

Jesus came to this world in the fullness of time to not be slack in giving salvation to all human beings before the angels in heaven who can't ever be more exact than Jesus who proved that to them in heaven when He cast Lucifer and his angels out of heaven in the fullness of eternity.

The devil fell from eternity with all his sins to enter into the time zone of burning up in hell one day with all who rebelled against God during their moment in time that was in the fullness of God grace for the great and small to repent and turn to Jesus to wash us clean in His precious blood.

All who ever lived before Jesus came to this world were covered in Jesus' fullness of time.

God's Word Will Never Change

A married couple can change on each other, but God's word will always be the same each and every day.

In every new year, the seasons will change, but no one can reason with God to change His holy word under the sun.

As we get older, our bodies will change from looking young to looking old, but God's word will never change like our bodies change in life.

We are living in a changing world where each generation goes through some changes in their lives that make them so different from the next generation, but God will never change His holy word forever and ever.

The day will change into the night and the night will change into the day, but God's holy word will never change on me and you.

You and I can change our minds at any time, but God will never change His holy word that can open our spiritually blind eyes to see that God is always so kind to show mercy on us who can be so sour in our love for God whose love is always so sweet to us.

Our feelings can change whether we're a Christian or not a Christian, but God will never change His holy word.

God's feelings will always stay the same, regardless of the hot, warm and cold weather of our lives.

God's word is superb over our days that won't change from being short under the sun, but time can change to make it too late for a lost soul to repent and turn to God.

If it's Not One Thing, It's Another Thing

If it's not one thing it's another thing.

If it's not another thing, it's always something that is going on, especially something bad, or so it seems.

You and I will go through one thing or another thing for doing the Lord's will that is always the right thing to do even when it comes to driving the speed limit on the road after the light turns green.

If it's not one thing, it's another thing from sunrise to sunset and from sunset to sunrise.

The Lord is merciful for you and me to lean on as we go through one thing and another thing that always seems to be going on, no matter who we are, great or small.

The devil will tempt us to do evil, no matter where we live.

If it's not one thing, it's another thing.

If it's not another thing to wake up out of our spiritual sleep, then it's always something especially bad that will come our way if we aren't living for the Lord who is never late to be there for you and me.

We should always be glad that the Lord Jesus Christ is always on time to rescue you and me.

If it's not one thing, it's another thing that we can see turning into something bad but whatever it is it is not too hard for the Lord to keep from giving you and me a brand-new start in our lives so we can love and obey Him who is above all things.

Sometimes We Can Move Too Fast

Sometimes we can move too fast and do something the Lord didn't tell us to do.

The Lord will never move you and me too fast to do anything, no matter where we live.

Whether we go here or there, we need to do what the Lord tells us to do.

Sometimes you and I can move too fast and say something the Lord didn't tell us to say, then we regret what we said in some kind of way because it can last for a long time in the ears of someone who may not forgive you and me.

Sometimes we can try to prove that we are right, but the Lord will never move you and me too fast to prove that we are right in anyone's eyes.

Sometimes we can move too fast to try to be on someone else's level of experience, but the Lord will never tell us to move too fast to try to be on someone else's level of experience — that may show us the devil's hand in it.

Sometimes we can move too fast and go somewhere, but the Lord will never tell us to move too fast to go anywhere.

Sometimes we can move too fast to go here and there, but the Lord will never tell us to move too fast on our toes to go here and there.

If we move too fast, we will sooner or later feel the bad effects of moving too fast without the will of the Lord.

My Ignorance

O Lord, You brought me from a mighty long way and set me on the mountaintop of Your holy word that is the best knowledge of truth to prolong my days.

My ignorance had begun to deteriorate when I heard Your holy word sounding so sweet in my ears, especially on Your holy Sabbath day of rest.

O Lord, You are forevermore higher than all the worldly knowledge that is very poor compared to the eternal riches of Your heavenly knowledge that is written in Your holy word for me to live by no matter where I am.

O Lord, You brought me from a mighty long way and put me in the sunlight of Your holy word for me to see today that my ignorance was darker than the darkest night.

O Lord, my ignorance handicapped my life for years and years because I just didn't know You and didn't care to know You.

You, O Lord, knew all of my heart all through my past ignorant years that today seem like years that never existed for me now that I love to hear and live by Your holy word instead of living in ignorance and fear.

O Lord, I am so glad that you winked Your eye at my ignorance that kept me in darkness.

I just didn't know I was ignorant, and the knowledge of the truth of Your holy word had passed by me.

No one convinced me to believe that there is a love beyond this world until Your holy word was revealed to me in church.

I now know that the love of God is forevermore and that ignorance has no voice to convince the wise that the knowledge of God's holy word doesn't make any good sense.

Just Downright No Good

The devil, whose name is Lucifer, was just downright no good for trying to exalt himself above God who is good all the time to you and me.

The devil was just downright no good for trying to find fault in God and cause the angels to believe that God is not love.

This caused the devil to be left out of all that God created on earth, especially the creation of man and woman below the heavens above.

The devil was just downright no good to the Son of God who was a man without sin in His flesh when he tried to tempt Jesus Christ for forty days and forty nights in the wilderness where Jesus did not sin against God.

The devil was just downright no good to make Jesus sacrifice His life and make it look so worthless when only Jesus can blot out all of our sins before God.

The devil is still just downright no good today as he preaches and teaches truth and error in the church and can sit amidst the congregation where you and I won't see him if we don't have the Holy Spirit to help us to stand up against him.

The word of God is like an iron rod that can't bend or break in our hands and we can use it to beat the devil throughout the land.

The devil will always be just downright no good, and that's not odd to God and all who love and obey God, who is just downright good to you and me all the time every day and every night.

We can come boldly to God through His Son, Jesus Christ, who makes our pleas before God in heaven forever beyond the devil who is just downright no good and will one day be gone forever like he never existed with his sins against God.

I Don't Have the Strength to Walk on My Own

I don't have the strength to walk on my own through the wilderness of life where the unknown preys on my soul all through the day and all through the night.

I don't have the strength to walk on my own through the swamp of life that can't wait for me to sink down in losing my hope.

O, my Lord, I can only walk through life on your strength that keeps me going strong in You day after day because I have no strength to call my own.

O Lord, Your strength is sweeter than the honey comb and more beautiful than the lily in the valley as I walk through the dark and narrow alley of life on Your strength that will never fail me.

I don't have the strength to walk so free through the wild jungle of life on my own two feet that can feel pain as I walk down the street.

O, my Lord and Savior Jesus Christ, Your strength stands me back up when I fall down into sin so I can repent and turn back to You and continue to walk through the broken promises of life on Your strength that the devil can't stalk and prey on any day or any night.

It's So Easy

It's so easy to feel one's own pain and be strong enough to bear it, but someone else might not be rough and tough enough to bear their pain.

It's so easy to get bent up and out of shape when someone says or does something that you and I hate.

It's so easy to not forgive someone, even if he or she is not aware of the bad effect of their words upon you and me.

It's so easy to only see all of the bad things that you and I are going through and not realize that someone else has been through the same things and gave Jesus Christ all of his or her trust, even if it was their last day to live.

It's so easy to want to be right in your own eyes, and it's so easy to say what you and I believe.

There is a God who can't lie to you and me who have eyes that can lie to us and mouths that can say words of disbelief for not yielding to the Holy Spirit on any day.

It's so easy to react in a negative way when you believe someone has set out to intentionally hurt you, but the reality is he or she just didn't know how you would respond to what they said to you.

It's so easy to only look out for yourself and claim to be self-made, but Jesus took on our blame that has guilt upon our names.

Jesus put himself aside and away from doing His will and instead did His Father's will to save us from our sins that are so easy to commit against God in our thoughts, words and actions.

Lost in Space

If you feel like you are lost in space, look forward to one day seeing Jesus on the clouds of glory with all of His holy angels answering your call to embrace you in an eternal holy place beyond the outer space.

You can feel like you are lost in space, especially when you are walking on the thin ice of life that can break on you and take you down into the blues that only Jesus can bring you through, no matter how lost you feel.

One day you and I will travel through the outer space on our way to heaven being so free from sin for being saved in Jesus Christ, who must have felt like He was lost in space when He was hanging on the cross to pay our cost.

That day gave the devil the blues because he knew he was a defeated foe because you and I would receive eternal life through Jesus Christ who fills up every space in heaven with God's will and love and joy.

Never Satisfied

My mind is never satisfied with thoughts, because God gave me a mind to think even if my thoughts are odd.

My heart is never satisfied with choices to make, because God gave me a heart to choose to make good or bad choices every day and reap what I sow.

My eyes are never satisfied with vision, because God gave me vision to see the results of my decisions that I make no matter what is my religion.

My ears are never satisfied with hearing, because God gave me ears to hear even things I don't agree with.

I have ears to hear about Jesus Christ, especially in church that Jesus is the head of to change my life for the better of humanity.

My life is never satisfied with living, because God gave me life to live unto Him until I go to the grave hopefully being saved in His Son, Jesus Christ, who will raise me up from the dead and take me to heaven like I never laid down in the grave before an eternal God who reigns forever in the highest heaven.

My mouth is never satisfied with words from the tip of my tongue, because God gave me a mouth to whip the devil with His holy word day after day that I can dive down into and get a drink of living waters to quench my thirst for lost souls to repent and turn to Jesus.

My nose is never satisfied with breath to breathe in and out of my nostrils for me to hopefully live until Jesus Christ comes back again in my lifetime for me to duck death.

Only I Can Have My

Only I can have my thoughts.

Only I can have my mouth to talk good or bad words.

Only I can have my motives.

Only I can have my intentions.

Only I can have my contentment.

Only I can have my feelings.

Only I can have my dreams.

Only I can have my eyes to see.

Only I can have my tongue to tame.

Only I can have my selfishness.

Only I can have my body.

Only I can have my life to live.

Only I can have my choices to make.

Only I can have my flaws.

Only I can have my mistakes.

Only I can have my fingers to write.

Only I can have my breath to breathe day after day.

Only I can have my ears to hear.

Only I can have my grudges.

Only I can have my forgiveness.

Only I can have my moment in time.

Only I can have my destiny.

Only I can have my peace.

Only I can have my hardships.

Only I can have my joy.

Only I can have my good days and bad days.

Only I can have my self-esteem.

Only I can have my achievements.

Only I can have my last day to live.

Only I can have my sow to reap.

Only I can have my wrongdoings.

Only I can have my actions days after day.

Only I can have my truth.

Only I can have my experiences.

Only I can have my desires.

Only I can have my lies.

Only I can have my doubts.

Only I can have my deceptions.

Only I can have my mouth to eat good or bad food.

Only I can have my hygiene.

Only I can have my health.

Only I can have my love to give.

Only I can have my hate.

Only I can have my victory in Jesus.

Only I can have my heart to give to Jesus.

Only I can have my relationship with Jesus.

Only I can have my trials for Jesus' name sake.

Only I can have my life to live for Jesus.

Only I can have my trust in Jesus.

Only I can have my existence to be about Jesus or be about the devil.

Only I can have my rebellion against God.

Only I can have my sins.

Only I can have my confession of sins.

Only I can have my repentance of sins.

Only I can have my hope in Jesus.

Only I can have my mansion in heaven.

Only I can have my humility unto Jesus.

Only I can have my praise unto Jesus.

Only I can have my thanks unto Jesus.

Only I can have my prayers unto Jesus.

Only I can have my worship unto Jesus.

Only I can have my choice to make Jesus my choice every day.

Through All of My Regrets

Through all of my regrets, I thank the Lord for giving me a second chance to repent and live my life unto Him.

Through all of my regrets, I thank the Lord for helping me to see how ignorant I was to not know that my soul is a precious gem to Him each and every day that I live my life.

Through all of my regrets, I thank my Lord and Savior Jesus Christ for giving me His mercy and grace that I don't deserve through all of my regrets that are no match for God's love being so superb above all of my regrets.

Jesus didn't allow my regrets to take me to the grave and allowed me to live to see this day.

Jesus has crushed all of my regrets under His foot, regardless of all who know me and can look and see my regrets in my life.

Today, the Lord is keeping me going strong in Him and gives me more and more of His blessings for loving and obeying Him beyond my regrets.

You and I will Usually Want To

You and I will usually want to talk to those who we know to be no stranger to you and me.

You and I will usually want to hang around those who we know to accept us for who we are from our heads down to our toes.

You and I will usually want to help those who we know to truly thank us for our help which is nothing new to me and you.

You and I will usually want to keep company with people who are like you and me, whether they are good or bad under the stars where you and I are good or bad in this world, very far below the heavens on high.

You and I will usually want to love those who are easy to love, day after day, even if they don't have a lot of words to say to you and me.

You and I will usually not want to be around those who are different from you and me wherever we go.

But, Jesus sat and ate with sinners who were different from Him, who gave birth to Christianity for all who were born in sin to repent and turn to God before our lives end.

Powerful Words

There are many people who speak powerful words, write powerful words and sing powerful words that are so right to many people every day and every night.

Many people have been changed for the better through somebody's powerful words, even written in a letter.

Many people have changed for the worst through somebody's powerful words that put a curse on their lives.

Many people have gone from rags to riches through somebody's powerful words that caused them to abandon hopelessness and kiss the ground he or she walked on before them.

No matter how many powerful words many people speak, their words will never be more powerful than God's holy word that can truly prolong anyone's life and cause them to leap for joy in the Lord while going through their trials and temptations.

Trials and temptations will never weaken you and me or give us an excuse to not choose to obey God's holy word that's filled with His ten golden rules.

No one's words in this world can be more powerful or change God's mind.

God gave you and me His holy word to live by, and God's Son, Jesus Christ, spoke and lived by those words under the sky before He went back up to heaven on high.

True Happiness

True happiness comes from loving Jesus.

True happiness comes from keeping our eyes on Jesus.

True happiness comes from putting all of our trust in Jesus.

True happiness comes from keeping Jesus' Commandments.

True happiness comes from holding onto Jesus on our good days and bad days.

True happiness comes from keeping our faith in Jesus.

True happiness comes from keeping our hope in Jesus.

True happiness comes from giving all of our heart to Jesus.

True happiness comes from denying ourselves and picking up our crosses to follow Jesus.

True happiness comes from winning souls to Jesus.

True happiness comes from working for Jesus.

True happiness comes from Jesus our all and all.

True happiness comes from humbling ourselves unto Jesus.

True happiness comes from repenting of our sins unto Jesus.

True happiness comes from being a new creature in Jesus.

True happiness comes from living our lives unto Jesus.

True happiness doesn't come from sinners like me and you.

True happiness comes from Jesus Christ, our Lord and Savior, who is the only One to save us from being lost in our sins if we believe in Him, which we can only do one day at a time.

True happiness comes from keeping Jesus first and above everyone and everything in this world.

True happiness comes from keeping Jesus first and above ourselves, which Lucifer and one third of the angels failed to do and were cast out of heaven and into eternal misery.

You and I can get true happiness in Jesus through our free will to choose Jesus over this sinful, miserable and uncertain world.

True happiness comes from praying to Jesus in the morning, noonday and in the night without ceasing.

True happiness comes from having a relationship with Jesus.

True happiness comes from Jesus making our burdens as light as a feather.

True happiness comes from Jesus giving us a peace of mind in this very troubled world.

True happiness comes from Jesus showing mercy on us and giving us His grace when we deserve to drop dead for even thinking an evil thought, which is a sin against Jesus Christ who is one with God and the Holy Spirit in the trinity Godhead in heaven where God said, "Let us create mankind in our image."

True happiness comes from Jesus Christ, who died on the cross for our sins and rose from the grave to give us the victory to die to self and rise up in His newness of life that we can truly be happy about for being like Jesus who the angels in heaven get their true happiness from forever and ever.

Only Jesus can
Create a New World

Only Jesus can create a new world, which He will do after the holy saints have been in heaven for a thousand years.

All the fancy and educated words of men and women can't create a new world.

All the genius and brilliant men and women can't create a new world.

The greatest technologies of men and women can't create a new world.

Only Jesus can do this and will do this after He destroys this old, sinful world in fire and brimstone that will burn up all the wicked and everything in this world.

All the wisdom and knowledge of men, women and boys and girls can't create a new world in their sins that all human beings were born into, causing them to have a sinful nature.

Only Jesus lived without sin in this sinful world, where He was born without sin in His flesh.

Only Jesus Christ, the Lord, can create a new world, not the skills, talents and inventions of human beings who have sinned and fallen short of the glory of God.

For thousands of years, human beings haven't yet made this world a perfect place to live, because today with the greatest technologies of human beings this world is still full of evil that only Jesus overcame.

Only Jesus can create a new world without any trace of evil that can corrupt the greatest minds and make them proud like Lucifer was up in heaven where he wanted to be God.

Many great and genius human beings have tried to create a new world and failed terribly, over and over again because human beings cannot do what Jesus can do.

Only Jesus has the power to create a new world that He will create after He burns up all sin in the lake of fire.

Can We Understand?

Can we understand the sin in our flesh that can cause us to think something we should not think?

Can we understand the sin in our flesh that can cause us to say something we should not say?

Can we understand the sin in our flesh that can cause us to want something that we should not want?

Can we understand the sin in our flesh that can cause us to feel something that we should not feel?

Can we understand the sin in our flesh that can cause us to go somewhere we should not go?

Can we understand the sin in our flesh that can cause us to hold something that we should not hold in our hands?

Can we understand the sin in our flesh that can cause us to eat some foods that we should not eat?

Can we understand the sin in our flesh that can cause us to have some motives we should not have?

Can we understand the sin in our flesh that can cause us to have some intentions that we should not have?

Can we understand the sin in our flesh that can cause us to wear something we should not wear?

Can we understand the sin in our flesh that can cause us to act the way we should not act?

Can we understand the sin in our flesh that we were born in to cause us to do something that we should not do?

The sin in our flesh cannot be fully understood by most genius people in this sinful world.

It took God giving us his only begotten Son, who had to leave heaven and come to this sinful world to save us from our sins.

Adam and Eve in all of their God-given perfection didn't know what they were getting themselves into for even touching that unforbidden fruit that God told them not to touch or eat in the midst of the Garden of Eden.

Can we understand the sin in our flesh that can cause anybody, even in the church, to turn away from the Lord, especially when the road gets rough and the going gets tough?

Only Jesus fully understands sin, because only Jesus didn't have sin in His flesh when He lived in this world among nothing but sinners like you and me.

It took God Himself giving up His only Son to shed His blood and die on a cross to save us from our sins that Jesus became on the cross to the fullest extent that God fully understood.

Jesus had to take on our sins so that you and I have no excuse to believe that Jesus can't cleanse us of our sins.

Even many people who go to church don't believe that Jesus can help them to overcome their weaknesses that come from sin in our flesh being a battle with our spirits every day.

Can we understand the sin in their flesh that can cause anyone to question God like Job did?

God had to ask Job, "Where were you when I laid down the foundations of the earth?"

Job was a perfect and upright man in the eyes of God, but he still had sin in his flesh.

Job didn't understand and questioned God in his hardships that God allowed the devil to bring upon him.

Can we understand the sin in our flesh that can cause anyone of us to be like Job's wife who told Job to curse God and die because she had died spiritually from the sins in her flesh that she didn't understand?

Her sins got the best of her, especially when she lost all of her children who she loved.

Can we understand the sin in our flesh that can cause us to deny Jesus before others, and believe we made ourselves prosperous?

We could not be who we are today without Jesus — we did not become who and what we are all by ourselves.

If we can truly understand the sins in our flesh that can catch us off guard at any time and anywhere, then we would truly know what it means to stay in prayer and humble ourselves before the Lord because sin can easily inject its venom of pride into us so we get a swelled head over what the Lord is doing for us.

We need to remember that we can't keep breath in our bodies and live our lives without the Lord's approval.

So, who are we sinners to understand the sin in our flesh that can cause us to get ill so unexpectedly and the doctors not even have a clue where the illness came from?

Jesus knows where the illness came from and can get rid of it for us, leaving the doctors amazed.

Can't Do More

Yesterday couldn't do more than what You, O Lord, allowed yesterday to do.

Today can't do more than what You, O Lord, allow today to do.

Tomorrow can't do more than what You, O Lord, allow tomorrow to do.

You and I can't do more than what You, O Lord, allow us to do.

All who are rich are rich because You, O Lord, allowed them to be rich.

All who are middle class and upper middle class are prosperous because You, O Lord, allowed them to be prosperous.

All who are lower middle class and poor are less fortunate because You, O Lord, allowed them to be less fortunate.

You and I are where we are in life because You, O Lord, allowed us to be where we are in our lives.

You and I can't go beyond what You, O Lord, allow us to go beyond.

Where we are in life right now is because You, O Lord, allowed us to be where we are in life right now, whether our life is good or bad.

Who are we to question the Lord, no matter what we have been through in our lives or whether we have brought hardships upon ourselves or not?

Our hardships can't do more to us than what You, O Lord, allow our hardships to do to us.

Our moment in time can't do more to us than what You, O Lord, allow our moment in time to do to us.

Nothing in this world can't do more to you and me than what You, Lord Jesus Christ, allow this world to do to anyone in this world.

If the Lord allows anyone or anything in this world to do more to us than what we can bear, then it is the Lord's reason that no one can override, no matter how rich and powerful they are in this world.

Our thoughts, words, feelings, reasons, ideas, opinions, theories, educated guesses, imaginations and actions cannot be more or do more than what You, O Lord, allow.

You, O Lord, are in charge of every day and are more loving and do more giving than sinners like me, who can only be saved in You, my Lord and Savior Jesus Christ.

The Greatest Reward

The greatest reward that anyone can ever receive is going back to heaven with Jesus when He comes back again on the clouds of glory.

That greatest reward will make all the rewards in this world look so worthless to all who are saved in Jesus Christ, the King of kings and Lord of lords.

The rewards in this world can look so good and can cause you and me to feel so good when we receive rewards from human beings, who don't have a heaven to put us in.

Receiving a good reward is never a bad thing, and no one would dispute this or turn down the reward.

Who in their right mind would turn down a reward for achieving something great in their life?

A bad person can receive a reward in this world from people who believe that he or she is doing something great.

A reward is evidence of an achievement that was made in the presence of others who see what you have done or what you are doing in their lives is a blessing to them and gives them something good to look forward to in their lives.

Our greatest reward is from the Lord, who wants to take us all back to heaven with Him when He comes back again on the clouds of glory.

But, we must choose to believe in Jesus Christ and love and obey Him in order to receive our eternal reward that will be great to all the angels in heaven, who will see our greatest achievement that came from believing in Jesus Christ.

There is no other greater choice that anyone can ever make than to choose to deny self and pick up one's cross and follow Jesus.

No one can ever give you and me a greater reward than Jesus Christ, who will reward us for going through trials for His holy name's sake.

The people of the world won't see our great reward from Jesus.

Even so-called Christians will believe that you and I are doing or have done something bad if we go through some hardships in our lives, just like Job's friends believed Job did something bad before God because he was going through hardships in his life.

The greatest reward that anyone can ever receive is going with Jesus back to heaven when He comes back again on the clouds of glory.

All that we go through for Jesus' holy name sake is to mold and shape us to receive our greatest reward that will be eternal beyond all the rewards in this world that is temporary and will one day pass away beneath the heavens on high where Jesus is eternal and will give us our greatest eternal reward for being saved in Him.

In Your Hands, O Lord

The past years were in Your Hands, O Lord who brought all the aged living people this far to see this day.

Every middle-aged and older man and woman should thank You, O Lord, for sparing their lives from an early grave.

The present days are in Your hands, O Lord, so that all who are alive, great and small, Christians and atheists, can know that there is a higher power beyond our mental and physical power.

We can be brought down by the power of the evils and unexpected dangers that can come our way on any day

The future is in Your hands, O Lord, and You know all who will be alive to be sealed in You to be changed from mortal to immortality in the twinkling of an eye and see You, O Lord, on the clouds of glory when You come back again.

The future is in Your Hands, O Lord.

You know all who will be alive and have the mark of the beast to be lost in their sins and drop dead when they see You on the clouds of glory.

The past, present, and future is in Your hands, O Lord.

You hold all existence together beyond this temporary world where grace is in Your hands that reach out and save a sinner who repents and turns to You, O Lord.

There is a Decree from Heaven

There is a decree from heaven to be passed down on earth.

That decree tells all human beings on earth to fear God and keep His Commandments.

That decree from heaven tells every human being to love one another and not make war with one another.

That decree from heaven tells every human being on earth to repent and turn to Jesus Christ, who every human being can believe in and be saved from being lost in our sins.

There is a divine decree from heaven to be passed down on earth for every human being to deny themselves and pick up their crosses and follow Jesus Christ, who is the way, the truth and the life to live day after day.

That decree from heaven tells every human being to come out of worshipping idols that have no heaven to put anyone into, only a hell to put every human being into.

That decree from heaven tells every human being on earth to love God with all of their minds, hearts, souls and strength day after day.

That decree from heaven tells every human being on earth to put all of their trust in Jesus Christ who will never fail any human being who trusts in Him.

That decree from heaven tells every human being not to lean to their own ways and do their own will, but to do the Lord's will even if it causes us to lose our lives because doing this will give us eternal life through Jesus Christ.

There is a holy and divine decree from heaven that has been passed down on earth for every human being to know that Jesus Christ is the only savior of the world and He will save every human being from their sins if they believe in Him.

There is a holy and divine decree from heaven being passed down on earth to every human being to have a chance to repent and turn to Jesus or reject Jesus before God closes His divine grace on this world .

It's moving very close to that day for God's decree in heaven to leave this world and ascend back up to heaven.

That decree from heaven passed down to every human being on earth is the bible scriptures that the Holy Spirit inspired holy men of God to write for every human being to know Jesus and live for Jesus by faith here on earth where the devil's decree is doom in hell's fire and brimstone.

A New Creature in Jesus Christ

When you and I become a new creature in Jesus Christ, there are people who will remind you and me of how we used to be.

They are threatened by the new you and me, especially if they see we are no longer down under them in poverty.

When you and I become a new creature in Jesus Christ, there are people who will get envious, especially if they see you and me moving up in life and no longer being immature and unintelligent.

They would rather see you and me the way we used to be.

When you and I become a new creature in Jesus Christ, there are people who will despise us for not being like them in their phony ways.

They don't like you and me being real about being a changed man or woman who has wised up and no longer does foolish things.

When you and I become a new creature in Jesus Christ, even so-called Christians will not like how the Lord is blessing you and me and making us shine brighter than them with our spiritual gifts in the church.

They will see our gifts as worthless to try to hide the fact that they are not giving Jesus their best efforts to build up the kingdom of God.

When you and I become a new creature in Jesus Christ, even some of our kinfolks won't like our changed life because they don't want to change from their own selfish ways and deny themselves and pick up their crosses and follow Jesus.

When you and I become a new creature in Jesus Christ, there are people who will never let go of the old you and me.

They would love to see the old you and me before their eyes instead of seeing you and me being like Jesus.

When you and I become a new creature in Jesus Christ, some of our worst enemies are the people who are the closest to us because they can't handle our changed life while they are stuck living in their sins.

When you and I become a new creature in Jesus Christ, there will be old friends from the past who show up in our lives and try to cause you and me to slip back into the sinful things we used to do with them.

When you and I become a new creature in Jesus Christ, we will have no desire to ever want to go back to living our past sins, but there are people who know how we used to be and will use our past lives against us.

They feel like they're worthy to judge and execute you and me with their unbelief and feel like we're not good enough to live a better life than them.

When you and I become a new creature in Jesus Christ, our Lord and Savior, no one can take that away from you and me no matter what they say about us.

You and I can choose to live for Jesus and shame the people who especially have a form of Godlessness that makes them deny the power of the Holy Spirit and be the same old carnal-minded creature day after day.

Being Married to Jesus

Being married to Jesus will not cause us to feel like Jesus is unfaithful to us.

Being married to Jesus will not cause us to feel like we can't trust Him.

Being married to Jesus will not cause us to feel like Jesus will abandon us.

Being married to Jesus will not cause us to feel like Jesus doesn't love us.

Being married to Jesus will not cause us to feel like Jesus is trying to control us.

Being married to Jesus will not cause us to feel like Jesus is ignoring us.

Being married to Jesus will not cause us to feel like Jesus doesn't want to listen to what we want to say to Him.

Being married to Jesus will not cause us to feel like Jesus is neglecting us.

Being married to Jesus will not cause us to feel like Jesus is changing on us.

Being married to Jesus will not cause us to feel like Jesus is pulling away from us.

Being married to Jesus will not cause us to feel like Jesus doesn't want to be with us.

Being married to Jesus will not cause us to feel like Jesus is irritated with us.

Being married to Jesus will not cause us to feel like Jesus has mood swings.

Being married to Jesus will not cause us to feel like Jesus is lying to us.

Being married to Jesus will not cause us to feel like Jesus is playing games with us.

Being married to Jesus will not cause us to feel like Jesus is putting us down.

Being married to Jesus will not cause us to feel like Jesus is trying to discourage us.

Being married to Jesus will not cause us to feel like Jesus is not giving us His support.

Being married to Jesus will not cause us to feel like Jesus is not patient with us.

Being married to Jesus will not cause us to feel like Jesus is just pretending with us.

Being married to Jesus will not cause us to feel like Jesus is dishonest to us.

Being married to Jesus will not cause us to feel like Jesus is not real with us.

Being married to Jesus will not cause us to feel like the marriage is over and done.

Being married to Jesus will not cause us to have ill feelings about Jesus.

Being married to Jesus will not cause us to have negative feelings about Jesus.

Being married to Jesus will not cause us to have bad feelings about Jesus, and if we do have bad feelings about Jesus, then we are not married to Him in our hearts even though we claim to be His church bride before the world.

A man can be married to a woman and not be faithful to her.

A woman can be married to a man and not be faithful to him.

That unfaithfulness can go on for years and years, and a spouse can ignore it like it doesn't exist in their marriage.

No one can be married to Jesus Christ and not believe in Him 'til death, but you will not part from Jesus you will only be asleep in Jesus who will wake you up when He blows His trumpet loud for you and me to come out of the grave and go with Him back to heaven for being His faithful church bride.

You and I can't claim to be married to Jesus if we don't keep His Commandments.

That is the real proof of our marriage to Him that the devil can't put asunder, nor can any human being or anything else in this world.

Not only a woman can be married to Jesus; a man can be married to Jesus Christ who is without sin and has no inclinations of unnatural affections.

Jesus didn't have unnatural affections toward any man when He lived in this world with no sin in His flesh.

You can be single and be married to Jesus, but it can't be that way with this world's standards because a single person can't be single and married at the same time.

Only Jesus can do the impossible that no one else can do.

True love and happiness will never decline for being married to Jesus.

Being married to Jesus is everlasting love that the angels in heaven and unfallen worlds will never turn their backs on.

Being married to Jesus is truly a miraculous and perfect marriage, and only a fool would divorce Jesus.

If

If luck could make our choices for us, then we would only live our lives by luck.

If our wishes could make our choices for us, then we would only live our lives by a wish.

If a dream could make our choices for us, then we would only live our lives by a dream.

If magic could make our choices for us, then we would only live our lives by magic.

If an accident could make our choices for us, then we would only live our lives by an accident.

If phenomenon could make our choices for us, then we would only live our lives by a phenomenon.

If a mystery could make our choices for us, then we would only live our lives by a mystery.

If an educated guess could make our choices for us, then we would only live our lives by an educated guess.

If an opinion could make our choices for us, then we would only live our lives by an opinion.

Before we were born into this world, luck was here waiting on us to choose to believe in luck and not believe in Jesus Christ.

Before we were born into this world, a wish was here waiting on us to choose to believe in a wish and not believe in Jesus Christ.

Before we were born into this world, a dream was here waiting on us to choose to believe in a dream and not believe in Jesus Christ.

Before we were born into this world, magic was here waiting on us to choose to believe in magic and not believe in Jesus Christ.

Before we were born into this world, an accident was here waiting on us to choose to believe in an accident and not believe in Jesus Christ.

Before we were born into this world, a phenomenon was here waiting on us to choose to believe in a phenomenon and not believe in Jesus Christ.

Before we were born into this world, a mystery was here waiting on us to choose to believe in a mystery and not believe in Jesus Christ.

Before we were born into this world, an educated guess was here waiting on us to choose to believe in an educated guess and not believe in Jesus Christ.

Before we were born into this world, an opinion was here waiting on us to choose to believe in an opinion and not believe in Jesus Christ.

If time could make our choices for us, then we would only live our lives by time.

If nature could make our choices for us, then we would only live our lives by nature.

If destiny could make our choices for us, then we would only live our lives by destiny.

If the devil could make our choices for us, then we would only live our lives by the devil.

Before we were born into this world, time was here waiting on us to choose to believe in time and not believe in Jesus Christ.

Before we were born into this world, nature was here waiting on us to choose to believe in nature and not believe in Jesus Christ.

Before we were born into this world, destiny was here waiting on us to choose to believe in destiny and not believe in Jesus Christ.

Before we were born into this world, the devil was here waiting on us to choose to believe in him and not believe in Jesus Christ.

Jesus Christ is one with God and Jesus was before all things seen and unseen that Jesus created, including everything in this world that didn't exist before Jesus.

We can believe in Jesus and live forever.

Jesus is waiting on you and me to enter heaven with Him when He comes back again on the clouds of glory.

Before we were born into this world, the Holy Spirit was here waiting on us to listen to His voice convicting us of our sins and waiting on us to confess our sins and repent and believe in Jesus Christ.

If God made our choices for us, then we would only live our life by a controlling God.

Before we were born into this world, God had predestined to give us His gift of the free will to make our own choices whether they are good or evil.

God just didn't leave us all alone with our choices, even though we will reap what we sow.

If death could make our choices for us, then we would be better off never having been born.

Before we were born into this world, death was here waiting on us to believe in death.

Many people will use the word death and say, "I am going to die one day anyway, so why not live my life like I want to live it?"

Jesus forever existed before death and Jesus will forever exist after death.

Jesus got the victory over death when He rose from the grave to show us that death is not the end in Him who we can believe in beyond this world of only temporary things that will one day pass away.

The Mysteries of Life

There are people who start out good in life and end up bad in life.

There are people who start out bad in life and end up good in life.

There are people who grew up in the church and then left the church.

There are people who didn't grow up in the church and will start going to church.

These are the mysteries of life.

There are people who are proud and achieve great accomplishments in their lives and then become drug addicts and homeless.

There are people who are labeled as failures and then they become rich and famous.

These are the mysteries of life.

There are people who talk loud and are intimidating and then they are as quiet as a mouse when they are around wise people.

There are people who are as quiet as a mouse and then talk a lot when they are around very loving and caring people.

These are the mysteries of life.

There are people who will give their last dollar to people they don't know and then be stingy to a loved one.

There are people who won't give even a penny to people who need it and then they will spend hundreds of dollars on their dog's vet bills.

These are the mysteries of life.

There are people who are takers and would take away the shoes off your feet and then they will sell them for maybe less than a dollar.

There are givers who will give away the shoes off their feet and then they will pray and ask the Lord to help that person do better in their lives.

These are the mysteries of life.

Jesus has also paid the high cost of the mysteries of life with His life and death on the cross.

This solved every mystery of life for you and me, because we know there is nothing in life that can override Jesus' reason to let us live to see another day.

This day is a mystery to destiny, which cannot solve the mystery of a repenting soul turning to Jesus today to be destined for eternal life.

The Show-Offs

The show-offs in this world love to be the center of attention.

The show-offs in this world are all about "me, myself and I."

The show-offs in this world have been deeply wounded by their bad experiences in life.

The show-offs in this world love and crave attention.

The show-offs in this world love to be in charge of everything.

The show-offs in this world just can't take no for an answer.

The show-offs in this world have been hurt a lot in their lives.

The show-offs in this world love to be number-one above all others.

The show-offs in this world love to cover up their weaknesses.

The show-offs in this world are truly afraid of failing at anything they do in their lives.

Back in the bible days, there were religious people who loved to show off their authority in the synagogues like the Pharisees and religious leaders did.

There are many show-offs in the churches today.

There are church folks who love to show off their knowledge of the bible scriptures but they have no real, genuine love for everybody in the church.

There are church folks who love to show off their presence in the church so that all eyes will be on them as soon as they walk through the church doors.

The worst show-offs are church folks who talk and walk like they made themselves to be prosperous in their lives, as if the Lord is beneath them.

The worse show-offs are church folks who believe they are the Lord's right-hand man or woman, as if the Lord can't do anything right without them.

The best thing that we church folks can show off to be a good thing is to show off how messed up we are to need Jesus who can save messed up people from our sins.

We church folks are no better than the show-offs in this world.

God loves everybody and shows off His love to all the world through His only begotten Son, Jesus Christ.

Only God is worthy to show off anything that He wants to show off.

No one can understand God's reasons, and they are forever pure with no pretense to show off His blessings upon you and me.

Quietness

Quietness can cause us to get a good night's sleep and wake up so refreshed in the morning light.

Quietness can heal a broken heart.

Quietness can ease a worried mind.

Quietness can wake up our dull senses.

Quietness can reveal the truth about someone to you and me.

Quietness can give us good ideas.

Quietness can encourage us to listen more and more to what is around us.

Quietness can truly cause us to listen to the voice of the Holy Spirit who we can understand so clear in a quiet place.

Quietness is from the Lord, who is quiet to listen to our prayers that can sound so noisy to the Holy Spirit, especially if trouble comes our way and we complain to the Lord in our prayers.

Quietness is a blessing to us from the Lord who loves a quiet soul that doesn't worry about anything because it knows He can work everything out for our good.

Quietness is like good medicine to take to get well because there is no illness in quietness because it can heal the mind and body.

Quietness can take us to the heart of God where we can rest our weary souls in God's love for us through His Son, Jesus Christ, who gives us some quiet time to meditate on His holy word.

There is No Way to Get Around the Lord's Holy Word

You and I can't talk our way out of getting around the Lord's holy word.

You and I can't think our way out of getting around the Lord's holy word.

You and I can't do anything to get our way out of getting around the Lord's holy word.

Jesus is Lord and Jesus is the word of God and no one can get around His holy word.

There is no way for anyone to get around the Lord's holy word.

No one's educated guess can get around the Lord's holy word.

No one's technology can get around the Lord's holy word.

No one's doctrines can get around the Lord's holy word.

No one's magic can get around the Lord's holy word.

No one's witchcraft can get around the Lord's holy word.

No one's bluff can get around the Lord's holy word.

No one's opinions can get around the Lord's holy word.

No one's luck can get around the Lord's holy word.

No one's success can get around the Lord's holy word.

No one's wealth can get around the Lord's holy word.

No one's education can get around the Lord's holy word.

No one's mind can get around the Lord's holy word.

No one's heart can get around the Lord's holy word.

No one's life can get around the Lord's holy word.

The Lord Jesus Christ is the word of God that was made flesh to live among sinners and save us from our sins if we confess and repent and turn to Him.

No one's dreams can get around the Lord's holy word.

No one can get around the Lord's holy word.

Many false prophets tried to get around the Lord's holy word back in the bible days, but they failed.

Many people today will try to get around the Lord's holy word with their traditional way of living by whatever was passed down to them from their parents and grandparents who tried to get around the Lord's holy word and got their results in nothing but a bad way.

You and I can't reason our way out of getting around the Lord's holy word that is all the truth about Jesus Christ, our Lord, who is one with God.

No one's choices can get around the Lord's holy word.

For no one can get around Him who even death could not get around.

Jesus rose from the grave, which could not keep Jesus from getting around to save us from our sins.

All of the devil's lies can't get around the Lord's holy word that is for you and me to live by and speak with love and power inside the church and outside the church.

No one can get around the Lord's holy word to try to rise above the Lord.

They will try and fail like Lucifer failed and was cast out of heaven.

There is no way to get around the Lord's holy word that came from the Holy Spirit who spoke words through holy men for even us today to live by because we can't get around the Lord's holy word.

Only a fool will try to get around the Lord's holy word, and they will fail miserably.

No one's genius can get around the Lord's holy word.

No one's power can get around the Lord's holy word.

No one's fate can get around the Lord's holy word.

There is no one in this world and there is nothing in this world that can get around the Lord's holy word because it was the word of God that spoke all things into existence and that word of God is the Lord Jesus Christ who no one can ever get around and live to tell about it.

In the Spiritual Deep Sleep

Many people are sleeping away in the spiritual deep sleep of holding grudges.

Many people are sleeping away in the spiritual deep sleep of telling lies.

Many people are sleeping away in the spiritual deep sleep of getting revenge.

Many people are sleeping away in the spiritual deep sleep of getting drunk.

Many people are sleeping away in the spiritual deep sleep of using drugs.

Many people are sleeping away in the spiritual deep sleep of having babies out of wedlock.

Many people are sleeping away in the spiritual deep sleep of being abusive.

Many people are sleeping away in the spiritual deep sleep of living in adultery.

Many people are sleeping away in the spiritual deep sleep of being controlling.

Many people are sleeping away in the spiritual deep sleep of being self-centered.

Many people are sleeping away in the spiritual deep sleep of being proud.

Many people are sleeping away in the spiritual deep sleep of being a phony.

Many people are sleeping away in the spiritual deep sleep of being a cheater.

Many people are sleeping away in the spiritual deep sleep of being a murderer.

Many people are sleeping away in the spiritual deep sleep of being a thief.

Many people are sleeping away in the spiritual deep sleep of being a rapist.

Many people are sleeping away in the spiritual deep sleep of being a child molester.

Many people are sleeping away in the spiritual deep sleep of abusing animals.

Many people are sleeping away in the spiritual deep sleep of selfishness.

Many people are sleeping away in the spiritual deep sleep of rebelling against God.

There are church folks who are sleeping away in the spiritual deep sleep of not returning faithful tithes and offerings unto the Lord.

There are church folks who are sleeping away in the spiritual deep sleep of complaining.

There are church folks who are sleeping away in the spiritual deep sleep of gossiping.

There are church folks who are sleeping away in the spiritual deep sleep of not doing the right things that they know to do right by God's holy word.

Especially we Christians know better than to be sleeping away in the spiritual deep sleep of the world because we are supposed to always be spiritually awake in the Lord and live by His holy word.

Especially we Christians know better than to be sleeping away in the spiritual deep sleep of the world because we are supposed to stay spiritually awake in our prayers and bible studies that will keep our spiritual eyes open to look upon Jesus who never sleeps on you and me.

We can always call on Him to walk with us through this spiritually deep sleeping world.

Only Jesus can guide us through this spiritual deep sleeping world where we can keep our spiritual eyes open by confessing and repenting of our sins and turning to Jesus one day at a time.

That is the only way to be spiritually awake in Jesus Christ in this spiritually deep sleeping world.

The Big Wheels of Time

The big wheels of time are rolling fast on the highway roads of one world order that is heading our way.

The big wheels of time will roll over all who are not giving Jesus any of their time in the household of faith where we assemble with the saints.

The big wheels of time are rolling fast on the racetracks of one world order that is coming our way all around the world where all of God's true Sabbath day keepers will get rolled over and flattened by the human agents of the devil.

The big wheels of time are rolling fast on the highway roads in the heart where only Jesus sees the real, true you and me beyond our good works and knowledge of His holy word.

The big wheels of time are rolling fast and will flatten all of the pretenders in the church who are just going through the motions of being a Christian but actually have no strong foundation to stand on against the hurricane winds of one world order.

That wind will surely blow us down to worship the beast whose mark will be on our hands to do the devil's work if we are not sealed in Jesus Christ.

The big wheels of time are rolling very fast on the highway roads of our free will choices in our knowledge of right and wrong and in our ignorance that time doesn't care about.

Time is running out fast, even for the righteous, who will be barely saved.

The big wheels of time are rolling very fast on the highway roads of the world, but they are not rolling fast enough to keep Jesus from sealing you and me in His victory over death to give us eternal life beyond one world order that will pass away while order in heaven will be forever for our good to worship our Lord and Savior Jesus Christ.

Believe in Jesus Christ

Believe in Jesus Christ, who can give us eternal life.

Many people believe in money that can't give us eternal life because money can come and money can go.

Believe in Jesus Christ, who can give us eternal life.

Many people believe in power that can't give us eternal life because power has corrupted many government officials.

Many people believe in the military that can't give us eternal life because the military can lose many soldiers in a war.

Believe in Jesus Christ, who can give us eternal life.

Many people believe in the doctor who can't give us eternal life because the doctor can give us the wrong medicine to take and make us sicker.

Many people believe in the aircraft pilot who can't give us eternal life because the aircraft pilot can have a crash landing.

Many people believe in their spouse who can't give them eternal life because a spouse can get very sick and die.

Believe in Jesus Christ, who is alive forever and ever to give us eternal life.

Many people believe in this world that can't give us eternal life because this world is filled with another day that is not promised to us to live.

Many people believe in themselves but they have no eternal life in them because of being born in sin to one day die and not exist anymore in the land of the living.

Believe in Jesus Christ, who can give us eternal life because Jesus is the origin of life in this world and all the other unfallen worlds and up in heaven that exists with life through Jesus Christ.

Jesus Christ is the self-existing one with God and the Holy Spirit who said, "Let us create man in our own image, in the image of God He Him: male and female — He created them.

Many people believe in the big bang theory that can't give us eternal life because many people have already died with their theories, while Jesus is alive and creating the new Jerusalem holy city for you and me to live in for believing in Him who gave the devil a big, hard bang of eternal death from his head down to his feet when Jesus rose from the grave.

Jesus is the Same Jesus Every Day

Jesus is the same Jesus every day, but you and I can change in some ways that we just don't see that we can change on Jesus and one another.

Jesus is the same Jesus every day and we are so blessed that Jesus doesn't change on us.

Jesus will not take us through any changes for the worst.

If Jesus takes us through any changes, it will always be for our good, but you and I can take one another through some changes for the worst if we don't love Jesus and keep His Commandments.

Jesus is the same loving Jesus every day.

Jesus' love for us won't decrease on us.

Only Jesus is the same Jesus every day, but you and I can decrease our love for others, especially if they hurt our feelings and they may not even know it.

Jesus is the same forgiving Jesus every day, and Jesus will forgive us of our sins if we confess and repent and turn to Him, which we need to do every day that we can sin against Jesus in a seen or unseen way.

Jesus doesn't need any time to think about forgiving us of our sins—He just does it right away—but you and I can need some time to forgive those who offend us.

Jesus is the same giving Jesus every day, and Jesus gives us everything that we need and even gives us some of our wants, but you and I can hold back on giving Jesus all of our hearts, which is what Jesus wants from us the most every day.

Jesus is the same healing Jesus every day, and Jesus heals us spiritually in His holy word, which is the very best medicine that anyone can take every day to be spiritually well and have the greatest wellness beyond our body that can be well and get sick.

When Jesus heals us spiritually, it has a much greater effect on us than any physical, mental, emotional and psychological healing that can recur with sickness, but spiritual healing from Jesus is permanent in our renewed life unto Jesus.

Jesus is the same Jesus every day, and the same Jesus forever and ever.

The devil knows this very well because he can't ever live in heaven again with Jesus, who cast him out of heaven forever and ever.

Jesus is the same Jesus Christ who will never change His holy word for anyone in heaven or anyone here on earth.

Jesus Truly Knows and the Devil Truly Knows

Jesus truly knows if you and I truly love Him and the devil truly knows if you and I truly love Jesus.

You and I don't truly know if we truly love Jesus because we can make a habit of only going through the motions with no real, true change in our hearts to compromise our faith in Jesus.

We can easily believe that we love Jesus, as long as things are going good in our lives.

Jesus truly knows and the devil truly knows if you and I truly love Jesus, but you and I don't truly know until our lives are in great danger and death is staring in our eyes like looking in the eyes of a poisonous snake close up.

One blink will cause that poisonous snake to bite us and kill us with its venom in a matter of minutes.

Jesus truly knows if you and I will truly love Him more than our loved ones, and the devil truly knows if you and I will love Jesus more than our loved ones.

Jesus truly knows that the devil can tempt anyone of our loved ones to cause you and me to dishonor Him, and the devil truly knows if he can tempt our most dear loved ones and make them cause you and me to deny Jesus with the truth that we know and don't live, especially in the presence of our most dear loved ones.

We can't get around Jesus and we can't get around the devil because Jesus and the devil want our souls — it's like a tug of war with Jesus pulling our right arms and the devil pulling our left arms.

We are standing in-between Jesus and the devil and we must choose which side we will lean over to in this tug of war over our souls day after day.

Jesus truly knows every day if you and I truly love Him, and the devil truly knows if you and I truly love Jesus.

You and I don't truly know if we love Jesus until real hard times come our way — that is the biggest test of our love for Jesus.

The only way that the devil truly knows if you and I love Jesus or don't love Jesus is the way the devil sees you and me living our lives unto Jesus or not living our lives unto Jesus today.

You and I can't fool Jesus and we can't fool the devil, but we can truly fool ourselves and one another in one way or another way because only going through the motions is so easy to do in our spiritually hereditary, sinful nature.

All that you and I have to do is want to choose to love Jesus for the Holy Spirit to take the rest of our steps to carry our love to Jesus, because we have no strength to love Jesus on our own and the devil truly knows that better than you and me.

Jesus Christ, our Lord and Savior, truly knows if you and I truly love Him, and the devil truly knows if you and I truly love Jesus or don't love Jesus.

If we don't pray to the Lord to keep His Holy Spirit in us, then we are like a slow turtle trying to cross a busy highway and are sure to get smashed up.

It's the same way with the devil who knows that he can smash us with his temptations if we don't have the Holy Spirit living in us to love Jesus with all of our minds, hearts, souls and strength.

Jesus truly knows if you and I truly love Him, and the devil truly knows if you and I love Jesus — not only out in public but also in the secrecy of our homes where many people live along.

The devil truly sees who loves Jesus and who loves him.

Jesus says, "If you love Me, you will keep My Commandments"

Jesus says, "If you love Me, you will keep My Commandments."

Jesus didn't say, if you fear me you will keep My Commandments.

Love and fear are two different things, because there is no fear in love.

If we keep the Commandments out of fearing the Lord, then we don't love the Lord.

If we keep the Commandments out of fear, then we are afraid of Jesus who is not about frightening anyone into keeping His Commandments.

Jesus wants us to keep His Commandments because of our love for Him, not because we fear what Jesus will do to us if we break His Commandments, and we do break them in one way or another way.

Parents want their children to obey them because they love their parents, not because they fear their parents.

Parents would truly accept love over fear, just like Jesus would truly accept love over fear.

If the parents know that their children love them and obey them, then the parents are sure without a doubt that their children are true to them even if the parents aren't living right before their children.

Parents usually know that love is more powerful than fear because they know that their children's love for them is a strong foundation they can stand on, even in their golden years.

Jesus is the same way, because Jesus wants you and me to truly love Him even if he doesn't answer our prayers on our time and may not give us all that we pray and ask Him for.

Jesus says if we love Him we will keep His Commandments.

Jesus didn't say if we fear Him we will keep His Commandments.

If a loving father and mother had to choose between their children loving them or fearing then, they would rather choose love because they love their children and no children should not fear their loving parents.

Even if many parents have a bad child, they also love that child.

Jesus is always so loving towards us, even though we are not always loving towards Him.

Jesus wants us to love Him and not fear Him because there is no fear in love.

If we obey Jesus out of fear, then we don't love Jesus.

Obeying Jesus out of fear is breaking His Commandments of love.

If Jesus didn't love us, He wouldn't have given us His Commandments to show us how to love Him and one another by God's holy standards for us to cherish down in our souls day after day.

No loving parent in their right mind would rather accept their children obeying them because of fear; they want them to obey them because they love them.

Why would anyone believe that Jesus would rather accept our fear making us obey Him over our love making us obey Him.

Jesus is not about wanting to control anyone to make them love Him.

Fear is all about controlling anyone to make them do what they don't want to do.

Jesus says, "If you love Me, you will keep My Commandments."

Back in the bible days, many Pharisees and religious leaders believed they could keep the Commandments without loving Jesus Christ.

Because of their envy towards Jesus, they didn't realize they were breaking the Commandments that Jesus originated.

Jesus gave Moses the Commandments He wrote with His fingers on the tablets up on Mount Sinai.

Jesus gave Moses His Commandments of love being for Moses and all the people to love Him and not fear Him.

There is No Time Left

There is no time left to be holding back the truth to people who don't know all the truth about the Lord's will for them to live by.

A lot of people want prayer, but prayer and obedience unto the Lord go together like a husband and wife who love each other.

There is no time left to be holding back the truth that the Lord wants you and me to tell to people with love.

There is no time left to be cutting corners with the truth of God's holy word that can set anyone free from the devil's lies.

There is no time left to be holding back the truth about Jesus Christ, who says, "If you love Me, you will keep my Commandments."

The devil will waste no time holding back his lies from you and me day after day.

If you and I know to do right, then we are supposed to do right because that is the truth by God.

The devil doesn't want you and me to tell the real, hard truth to people who are living in their sins, whether they are ignorant about the truth or if they know the truth and are not living the truth of God's holy word.

There is no time left to be holding back the truth when the Lord gives you and me the opportunity to tell the truth to people with love.

If we do this, people have no excuse to believe that they can walk away from the truth and not regret it sooner or later down the road.

Many people want prayer, but they don't want to accept the truth that you and I tell them to set them free from that old lying devil who hates for you and me to speak God's holy word of truth to anyone who is living in the darkness of their sins.

There is no time left to hold back the truth that many people see as unpleasant because they are holding back their hearts from God.

They are not denying self and they are not picking up their cross to follow Jesus Christ.

If you and I hold back the truth that people need to hear, then we deny Jesus before them because Jesus is the truth to save us from our sins if we repent and turn to Him in every way.

There is no time left for anyone to be half-stepping on Jesus.

You and I have no time left to be silent with the truth about Jesus' will for people to do, because the devil will not keep silent about his lies day after day.

Jesus will never half-step on anyone to save us from our sins.

No one can truly stand on that they have some time left to see another day without Jesus' approval.

There is no time left for anyone to neglect their borrowed time given to all of us to choose to love and obey Jesus like it's our last day to live.

Who Can Understand God's Decisions?

Who can understand why God allows men who we are not in favor of to be president of the United States of America?

Who can understand God's decisions?

It's impossible for human beings to understand God's decisions.

Who can understand why God allows a wicked man and woman to live a long life and a good man and woman to live a short life?

Many wicked people live a long life and many good people live a short life under the umbrella of God's decisions.

Who can understand God's decisions?

Even the angels in heaven and the unfallen worlds can't figure out why God allows little babies to be killed so they don't live and grow up into adults who can choose to do good or evil.

If we could understand God's decisions then we would truly know that God can never be wrong about whatever decision He makes.

If we could understand God's decisions that no one can override, then we would truly know our decisions can't be right without God's approval of our decisions.

Who can understand why God allows a fool to deceive millions of people and make them believe him?

Who can understand why God allows a sheep in wolf's clothing to preach in the pulpit in the church among His true remnant children?

It's impossible for even us church folks to understand God's decisions.

We can believe we know God so very well and will be disappointed if God doesn't answer all of our prayers that may not be in God's will to grant us.

Who can understand God's decisions?

Even Jonah didn't understand why God wanted him to go to Nineveh to tell the wicked people to repent, and he didn't obey God and got on a ship.

He had to face God again, and God had Jonah thrown into the sea and a whale swallowed him down into its belly.

Jonah didn't understand God after that experience until he cried out to God to set him free from the belly of the whale after he'd been there for three days.

Jonah realized then that he had to obey God, even if he didn't understand why God decided to tell him to go to Nineveh to tell the wicked people to repent and turn to God.

God's Precious Jewels

God has His precious jewels in the prisons.

God has His precious jewels on the city streets.

God has His precious jewels in the psychiatric hospitals.

God has His precious jewels in the projects.

God has His precious jewels in the ghettos.

God has His precious jewels on the battlefields.

God has His precious jewels all around the world.

God has His precious jewels in every church.

God has His precious jewels in every city.

God has His precious jewels in every town.

God has His precious jewels in every state

God has His precious jewels in every country.

God has His precious jewels in every culture.

God has His precious jewels in every color of the skin.

God has His precious jewels in every age.

God has His precious jewels in class of people.

God has His precious jewels in every language of people.

God has His precious jewels in race of people.

Many people in the church will define their precious jewel to be rich and famous and will look down on the poor like they are rotten food for swine to eat.

God shows no respect of persons to be His precious jewels that you and I can easily overlook and consider to be less important, even in the church.

We Have to get Tough with the Devil

We have to get tough with the devil because if we don't, the devil will walk all over us with his control techniques.

The devil has his human agents who he uses to try to control you and be and put us under his spell.

If you and I stay in prayer without ceasing, the Holy Spirit will give us the power to tough it out with the devil and his human agents who could be right in our family.

The devil loves to prey especially on weak Christians who are afraid to speak up against his lies that cause spiritual adultery that can surely lead to physical adultery.

We have to get tough with the devil who is all about holding grudges and loves to use his human agents to hold grudges even over the smallest arguments that won't kill anyone.

We have to get tough with the devil, who loves to see you and me being spiritually weak so that he can use his human agents to rub our flaws in our faces and use them against us as if they are so perfect to have no sins.

We have to get tough with the devil, who loves to catch us off guard and attack us with his angry human agents who know that the truth of God's holy word is too tough for them to take in when you and I hit some nerves in them.

We have to get tough with the devil and we can't do that without the Lord on our side to give us the strength and the wisdom to back the devil up into a corner with his human agents and make them look so foolish for trying to manipulate you and me who are God's chosen ones for loving Jesus and keeping His Commandments.

You and I Must Go Through Some Hardships

You and I must go through some hardships for Jesus' name sake to build a relationship with Jesus, and that won't come easy.

There are church folks who only want an easy spiritual cruise ride on their Christian journey with the Lord, but they don't' want to ride on any spiritual bumpy roads for Jesus' name sake.

There are church folks who will only talk about losing some spiritual heavy weight for Jesus' name sake, but they don't want to go through any rigorous spiritual exercises for Jesus' name sake.

You and I must go through some hardships for Jesus' name sake.

There are church folks who want to be in the spiritual limelight and have a great name in the church, but they don't want to be a spiritual janitor and do the hard work behind the spiritual curtains for Jesus' name sake.

There are church folks who want to sit at the spiritual banquet table with Jesus, but they don't want to share any of their spiritual food with others for Jesus' name sake.

You and I must go through some hardships to have a relationship with Jesus Christ.

There are church folks who want to be powerful spiritual leaders in the church, but they don't want to go the extra mile to help someone in great need for Jesus' name sake.

There are church folks who want to be the lawyer, jury and judge in the church, but they don't' want to admit their guilty flaws before others for Jesus' name sake.

You and I must go through some hardships for Jesus' holy name sake to have a relationship with Jesus.

Jesus went through some hardships that cost Him His life because He wanted to have a relationship with the human race to save us from our sins.

The devil hates for us to have a relationship with Jesus because he knows that Jesus loves us and wants to have a relationship with us day after day.

If you and I call ourselves Christians and are not going through any hardships for Jesus' name sake, then we are only a puppet on a string for the devil who is making us a laughing stock before his demons and his human agents.

If you and I have a relationship with Jesus, it's because we have been through some hardships for Jesus' name sake and are still going through some hardships today with joy still in our hearts because we know from experience that Jesus cannot fail to give us the victory over any hardships we go through for His holy name sake.

If Your Heart is Broken into a Thousand Pieces

If your heart is broken into a thousand pieces, give it to Jesus and ask Him to give you the strength to bear the pain.

If you give your broken heart to Jesus, you can let your pain take its full course at full speed ahead and let your tears fall into Jesus' loving hands and He will hold your sadness so dear to Him.

You can cry out to Jesus with all of your might and He will truly feel your every sad emotion and strengthen you for trusting Him to open all of your heart-felt pain before His healing open arms.

You can't trust anyone else more than you can trust Jesus, who knows without a doubt how to put together a thousand pieces of your broken heart.

Time can't do better at mending your broken heart than Jesus, who knows that time is so broken in this sinful world.

Whatever way your heart and my heart get broken into a thousand pieces, only Jesus sees all of the pieces and will pick them up with his fingers of love to put you and me back together and give us a heart of joy like we were never broken up into a thousand pieces.

If you and I believe that we can mend our own broken hearts, then we will break our hearts into many more pieces by holding onto bitterness and unforgiveness in our hearts.

You and I can cut up our own cross to bear for wallowing in the broken thousand pieces of our hearts that we can choose to give to Jesus, no matter if our emotional pain is raging like a tidal wave.

There is no pain that is too much for Jesus to ease and comfort, but you and I can make it so hard on ourselves by trying to sweep a thousand broken pieces of our hearts under a rug of pride.

If your heart is broken into a thousand pieces of sharp glass, you can only trust Jesus to pick it all up without losing one piece and without getting cut from the smallest to the biggest pieces of glass from your broken heart.

Your thousand pieces of broken glass from your heart and my heart can surely cut up others who will try to pick up our broken thousand pieces and can surely dump them back on you and me along with their thousand pieces of broken heart that only Jesus can pick up without ever getting cut up.

If your heart is broken into a thousand pieces and if my heart is broken into a thousand pieces of grief, doubt and fear, we should give it all to Jesus, whose heart was broken into more than a thousand pieces when God had forsaken Him on the cross that Jesus became sin on in our place to save us from our broken sins.

Across the Countless Galaxies

One day soon, Jesus will come back again on the clouds of glory to take us to His banquet in heaven.

When this happens, we will travel with Jesus and all the angels across the countless galaxies.

At Jesus' magnificent banquet in heaven there will be unlimited seats so all the holy saints can sit down around God's banqueting table.

As we travel with Jesus back to heaven across the countless galaxies, we will enter into His holy Sabbath day of rest beyond all of the temporary banquets here on earth that are only a shadow of the real, glorious banquet in heaven.

We can only assume what Jesus' banquet will be like until we gratefully walk through the everlasting gates in heaven and hopefully see our names written in pure gold on the blissful seats that we will hopefully sit down on with unspeakable joy and unspeakable admiration.

No pain, heartaches, tears or grief will exist upon us as we travel with Jesus Christ, our Lord and Savior, across the countless galaxies to get to Jesus' vibrant and captivating banquet where our names are engraved on the banqueting table because of us being saved in Jesus Christ.

Jesus will be our eternally royal crown heavenly host who will speak on all the holy saints' behalf for believing in Him who foreknew before we were born who will be at His dazzling banquet.

While we travel with Jesus on our way across the majestic galaxies, heading toward God's omnipotent grand opening banquet in heaven, the unfallen worlds will be happily standing by and watching us with great wonder on their faces because they will see our joy filling up all the countless galaxies.

One day soon, Jesus is coming back again on the clouds of glory to take us all to His banquet in heaven.

As we travel with Jesus and all the angels and all the holy saints, the infinite galaxies will marvel at us for shining so bright in Jesus' eternal light that will shine all around us to illuminate the universe.

Loving Jesus and keeping His Commandments will eternally seal our reservations in our minds for us to one day travel with Jesus across the vast galaxies to get to that radiant and miraculous banquet that will greatly cheer the unfallen worlds with unmeasurable gladness to hover over all of our earthly banquets, bringing us together on one accord in Jesus' holy name.

Will Move On Into

The seconds will move on into a minute.

The minutes will move on into an hour.

The morning will move on into the afternoon.

The afternoon will move on into the evening.

The evening will move on into the night.

The days will move on into a week.

The weeks will move on into a month.

The months will move on into a year.

The years will move on into a decade.

The decades will move on into a century.

The centuries will move on into a millennium.

The ounces will move on into a cup.

The cups will move on into a pint.

The pints will move on into a quart.

The quarts will move on into a gallon.

The inches will move on into a foot.

The feet will move on into a yard.

The yards will move on into an acre.

The summer will move on into the fall.

The fall will move on into the winter.

The winter will move on into the spring.

The spring will move on into the summer.

A true child of God will move into winning souls unto Jesus Christ.

A true child of God will move into going through trials for Jesus' holy name sake.

True children of God will move into unspeakable joy beyond the fiery dots of disappointments thrown at them.

Living for Jesus Christ, our Lord, will move on into living forever and ever one day soon when Jesus comes back again on the clouds of glory.

Living for the devil will move into the lake of fire and brimstone for all the wicked who are lost in their sins.

A true child of God will move on into eternal life in Jesus Christ.

No one in this sinful world can give us eternal life to move on into living in the new Jerusalem holy city that has streets made of pure, everlasting gold, only Jesus can do that for us.

The Devil's Most Busy Day

The devil's most busy day is God's holy Sabbath day of rest that God created for all men to rest from their labor and work.

The devil's most busy day is Saturday, being the seventh day of the week and the memorial day of all God's creation.

If the devil knows that he can cause you and me to not keep the Sabbath day holy unto God, then he pretty much has us where he wants us to be.

The Lord Jesus Christ kept the Sabbath day holy when He lived in this world with no sin in his flesh.

The devil's most busy day of the week is Saturday that he causes many people to lean to their own ways of working on their jobs, going to the stores and shopping malls.

The devil's most busy day of the week is Saturday and that is when the devil loves to cause many people to go to football games, basketball games, baseball games, hockey games and parties.

The devil's most busy day is Saturday and the devil loves to cause many people to go to weddings, funerals and just stay at home and maybe sleep all day.

The devil knows that if he can cause you and me to break the Sabbath, then he can cause us to do very much our own will and not God's will.

God's will is for us to keep the Sabbath day holy, but the devil hates for anyone to keep the Sabbath holy.

The devil's most busy day of the week is Saturday, which is God's holy Sabbath day of rest for all people around the world.

The Lord says that we can do good things on the Sabbath day of rest. We can help people who are in need of things like medical care.

This would be like getting the ox out of the ditch on God's holy Sabbath day of rest.

There are people who believe that they can keep every day holy.

We can live a holy life every day, but we can't keep every day holy because if that was true then God would not have given man even one day to work.

God gave man six days to work and the seventh for the holy Sabbath day of rest.

The holy Sabbath day is Saturday because it's the seventh day of the week that God rested from all of His creative works.

God really didn't need to rest because God never gets tired, but God knew that man would need to take a day off to rest from six days of work.

God foreknew that we would dig our own graves if He allowed us to work seven days a week and have no time off.

So, he wants us to spend a day with Him, and we truly need to spend a day with our creator God in the household of faith.

The devil's most busy day of the week is Saturday, the day God set apart from the other six days for us to rest our bodies and minds from working for human beings who have no heaven to put anyone into.

The devil's most busy day is Saturday, and the devil loves to be worshipped on that day because he knows that if he can cause so many people to break the Sabbath then he can turn them away from God.

Even on the calendar of men, Saturday is the seventh day of the week, and the devil knows very well and doesn't want you and me to keep the Sabbath day holy unto God.

Saturday is the devil's most busy day that he sets the pace for anyone to do his evils against God who made the Sabbath for man to keep holy.

God won't hold people accountable for what they don't know about Saturday being the holy Sabbath day of rest.

God has other sheep who are not in His sheep fold and they will keep the Sabbath on the way back to heaven where keeping the

Sabbath will be forever and ever kept, along with keeping all the other Commandments of God.

The devil's most busy day is Saturday, that he causes many people forget about God's memorial day of all His creation.

God's most busy day is Saturday because that is when God meets with all the angels in heaven and all the unfallen worlds who join in with us Sabbath keepers on earth where God made the Sabbath for all human beings to keep on Saturday.

The devil truly knows that if he can cause anyone to believe that Sunday is the Sabbath, then he doesn't have to burn in hell for their refusal to keep the Sabbath if they know to keep it on Saturday.

The Lord says, "Remember to keep the Sabbath day holy."

God set that day apart from the other six days in the week that God didn't command us to remember to keep holy even though God wants us to live a holy life unto Him every day for us to be different from the people of the world to see us being like Jesus seven days in the week.

God commands for all men to take only one day off from work to spend worshipping Him and giving Him all the glory and praise for all that He does for us.

The devil loves to keep who he can keep busy seven day a week so they spend no time with God in the household of faith where the origin of the church began on Saturday, the seventh day of the week.

We are supposed to assemble ourselves together to worship God in spirit and truth on Saturday.

There is no truth in Sunday being the holy Sabbath day of rest.

Sunday comes from pagans worshipping the sun as their god.

The devil's most busy day is Saturday and he won't forget to try to cause anyone to turn their foot away from the Sabbath being Saturday, the seventh day of the week, even on the calendar of men.

If God was Not Miraculous

If God was not miraculous, then we all would have no clean air to breathe, because if God let the devil have his every way there would be air pollution all over this world.

It's a miracle from God that there is still some clean air for many of us to breathe in and out of our nostrils.

If God was not miraculous, then there would be no marriages between a man and a woman, because if God let the devil have his every way there would be nothing but same-sex marriages.

It's a miracle from God that the marriage between a man and a woman still exists today all around the world where same-sex marriages are rampant.

If God was not miraculous, then every animal would attack every human being, because if God let the devil have his every way all the animals would be possessed by the devil which would cause them to be against all human beings.

It's a miracle from God that most of the animals fear us human beings because God put that fear in them after Adam and Eve sinned against God.

God put that fear in the animals to protect the human race from getting devoured by the animals that Adam passed sin down to when all the animals were so innocent and did not deserve it.

If God was not miraculous, then no human beings would be in their right minds, because if God let the devil have his every way all human beings would be insane and not be able to make any good choices, especially not being able to make Jesus our choice.

It's a miracle from God that many of us human beings are in our right minds to make good choices every day, which the devil hates because making good choices is from the Lord God.

If God was not miraculous, then no human being would be alive today, because if God let the devil have his every way he would possess every human being and make us kill one another so we have no way to enter into heaven.

God says, "Thou shalt not kill," in one of His Commandments to show and tell that there won't be any murderers in heaven.

If God was not miraculous, then God would let the devil have his every way to possess men of war in every nation so they would shoot off their nuclear warheads against one another.

It's a miracle from God that the human race still exists today from coast to coast.

If God was not miraculous, everybody would get in an accident on the roads, because if God let the devil have his every way on the roads then he would possess every driver and make them run into each other so there would be no survivors on the local and highway roads.

It's a miracle from God that even some reckless drivers make it back home safely when they know that they deserved to have been in an accident and die.

If God was not miraculous, then the church would be so worthless to go to and it would be a waste of time to assemble ourselves together because it would be a lost cause.

It's a miracle from God that He gave us His only begotten Son to save us from our sins for us to be His church body that Jesus is the head of to be so miraculous to the angels in heaven for the devil to be a defeated foe.

The Truth is the Best Thing

The truth is the best thing to encourage anyone to wise up and do better in life.

The truth is the best thing to help anyone to face up to reality to not want to escape into a fairy tale.

The truth is the best thing to set anyone free from believing lies and living a lie.

The truth is the best thing to open up anyone's eyes to see someone for who they really are.

The truth is the best thing to speak from the tip of anyone's tongue.

The truth is the best thing to bring out the best in anyone who will accept the truth spoken to them.

The truth is the best thing to show anyone who loves them or hates them.

The truth is the best thing to hold onto from day to day.

The truth is real proof about everyone's life.

The truth is the best thing to believe from day to day.

The truth is the only way to be right about what we say.

The truth is the best thing to choose from day to day.

The truth is good and a lie is evil.

The truth is the best thing to heal anyone's broken heart and mend it to move onto someone who truly loves you.

The truth is the best thing to make anyone guilty of whatever we say wrong and do wrong.

The truth is the best thing to the Lord, who will accept true confessions and repentance from anyone who wants to turn to Him.

The truth is the best thing that anyone can speak and live unto the Lord, even if our life is in the shadow of death that has no power over the truth about Jesus Christ who got the victory over death and the grave to give anyone eternal life for believing in him who is the way, the truth and the life.

The truth is the best thing that is written in the bible that many people don't believe but the devil can deceive anyone's five senses that a fool will believe in when Jesus is the origin of the truth to fulfill bible prophecy that science can't do down to the end of this world.

The truth is the best thing to live by from day to day under the sky where there is no truth in the devil who hates the truth.

The truth is the best thing to get rid of illusions and delusions that many church folks bring with them to church that Jesus Christ is the head of to perform spiritual surgery on anyone's heart and cut out the cancers of the devil's lies to renew anyone's life to live the truth of a new creature in Him.

If You and I Make it to Heaven

If you and I make it to heaven, that will truly be only through Jesus Christ who we must believe in to be saved and receive eternal life.

If you and I make it to heaven, we may very well go and visit the unfallen worlds and talk to terrestrial beings who may tell us how close they may have come to giving into the devil's temptations.

If you and I make it to heaven, we may very well talk to all the angels who may very well tell us how close they may have come to listening to Lucifer's lies and rebelling against God in heaven.

If you and I make it to heaven, we may very well travel through billions of galaxies and study them all throughout billions of universes.

If you and I make it to heaven, we may very well study all the unfallen worlds that may be in billions of universes.

If you and I make it to heaven, we may very well get to know the names of every angel when the bible only has a few names of the angels.

If you and I make it to heaven, we may very well get to know everyone's name in heaven where we will be forever learning more and more about our Lord and Savior Jesus Christ, who created all things in heaven and earth.

We may very well travel faster than the speed of light from the highest heaven, where God is into the billions of universes, to join all the unfallen worlds in worshipping God and giving God all the glory and praise along with all the angels in the highest heaven.

If you and I make it to heaven, we may very well see many different kinds of animals that we've never seen in this sinful world.

If you and I make it to heaven, we may very well get to know the names of every animal and even talk to all the animals that won't misunderstand one word that we say to them.

If you and I make it to heaven, we may very well speak the same language that all the unfallen worlds speak as well as the angels speak.

If you and I make it to heaven, we may very well speak one language like it was before the flood that only Noah and his wife and three sons and their wives lived through for obeying God's command for them to get into the ark.

If you and I make it to heaven, we may very well get to learn the technology and science in the unfallen worlds that may very well make the greatest technology in this sinful world look so old and out of date.

Jesus has already proven that this technology in this world doesn't come anywhere close to Him who walked on water, calmed the storm, fed thousands of people with five loaves of bread and two fish, and Jesus raised the dead and ascended back up to heaven where no jet or airplane or spacecraft ever flew to.

If you and I make it to heaven, we may very well see Jesus creating miraculous things that we could have never imagined on earth where sin has corrupted and dwarfed our bodies and imaginations to be so small in stature and mind.

If you and I make it to heaven, we may very well say to Jesus, "I am so glad that You are the only One to judge everybody's hearts."

You and I can only want someone to make it to heaven, but Jesus knows if they are not one of His own, no matter how holy and righteous they appear to you and me.

Prayer is a Lifestyle for Every Christian

Prayer is a lifestyle for every Christian who is supposed to pray to Jesus without ceasing.

Prayer is a lifestyle like wearing clothes every day.

Prayer is a lifestyle like wearing shoes on our feet every day.

Prayer is a lifestyle like combing our hair every day.

Prayer is a lifestyle like taking a shower every day.

Prayer is a lifestyle like brushing our teeth after every meal.

Prayer is a lifestyle like exercising every day.

Prayer is a lifestyle like putting on some clean clothes every day.

Prayer is a lifestyle like for every Christian to pray to Jesus every day that we live.

We can never pray to Jesus enough to be like not having enough clean air to breathe in and out of our nostrils.

Prayer is a lifestyle for every Christian to pray to our Lord and Savior Jesus Christ like getting some sunlight that we need every day to energize us.

Without prayer to Jesus, no one can be like Jesus who stayed in prayer unto His heavenly Father God when Jesus lived in this world without sin in His flesh.

Without prayer to Jesus, no one can be a Christian who originated through Jesus Christ who we must believe in to be a Christian and be saved in Jesus Christ.

We would be so spiritually weak every day if we don't pray to Jesus who the Holy Spirit takes our prayers up to for Jesus to hear us and strengthen us.

Spiritual strength is the strength that we need from day to day to resist the devil's temptations.

Prayer is a lifestyle for every Christian to pray to Jesus, not only for themselves but also for everyone to give up their old, sinful lifestyles and repent and turn to Jesus.

Jesus made prayer His lifestyle when He lived in this sinful world where everyone was born in sin except Him to save all men from their sins.

Prayer is a lifestyle for every Christian to pray to Jesus without ceasing like always locking our doors to secure ourselves and everything that we have in our houses, which is our most private place next to our hearts every day.